To Mei Lien: she married 30 years ago a human being who in the intervening years turned into a lawyer, accountant, and, perhaps worst of all, a writer.

Consumer

Law

FOURTH EDITION

PETER M WALKER
LLB (LOND), FFA, FIAB, MISM
BARRISTER, LINCOLN'S INN

SERIES EDITOR
CM BRAND, SOLICITOR

Cavendish
Publishing
Limited

Fourth edition published in Great Britain 2001 by Cavendish Publishing Limited, The Glass House, Wharton Street, London WC1X 9PX, United Kingdom

Telephone: +44 (0)20 7278 8000   Facsimile: +44 (0)20 7278 8080

Email: info@cavendishpublishing.com

Website: www.cavendishpublishing.com

© Walker, P 2001

British Library Cataloguing in Publication Data

Walker, Peter M
Consumer law – 4th ed – (Practice notes series)
1 Consumer protection – law and legisaltion – England
I Title
343.4'1'071

ISBN 1 85941 573 3

Printed and bound in Great Britain

Contents

1 Basic Information   **1**

  1.1   Consumers and suppliers   1

  1.2   Definition of 'consumer'   1

  1.3   Sources – statutes   2

  1.4   Statutory instruments and the EU influence   2

2 Interviewing the Consumer-Client – Sale of Goods and Services   **5**

  2.1   Introduction   5

  2.2   Consumers' questionnaire   6

  2.3   Completing the questionnaire   7

  2.4   Follow-up (subject to the client's instructions)   8

  2.5   Letters – the right style   8

  2.6   Precedent letter to seller   9

3 Interviewing the Seller-Client – Sale of Goods and Services   **11**

  3.1   Introduction   11

  3.2   Suppliers' questionnaire   12

  3.3   Follow-up (subject to the client's instructions)   13

4 Common Problems in Contract   15

   4.1   Formation of the contract   15

   4.2   Misrepresentation   16

   4.3   Advertising   16

   4.4   Deposits and prepayments   17

   4.5   Ownership   17

   4.6   Quality   18

   4.7   Avoiding liability   18

   4.8   Consumer credit   19

   4.9   Time   19

   4.10   Delivery and acceptance   19

   4.11   Instruction books   20

   4.12   Gifts and privity   20

   4.13   Guarantees   21

   4.14   Limitation of liability   21

   4.15   Particular problems with standard form contracts   23

   4.16   Holidays   23

   4.17   Loss of enjoyment, generally   23

5 Common Problems in Tort   25

   5.1   Negligence   25

   5.2   Product recall   26

   5.3   Economic loss   27

   5.4   Product liability under the Consumer Protection
       Act 1987   27

   5.5   Defences under the Consumer Protection Act 1987   28

   5.6   Detention of goods   29

| 5.7 | Uncollected goods | 30 |
| 5.8 | Advising suppliers on their own procedures | 31 |

6 Litigation – Sale of Goods and Services — 33

6.1	Introduction	33
6.2	Alternatives to courts	33
6.3	Contractual arbitration clauses	34
6.4	Alternative dispute resolution	34
6.5	Which court?	34
6.6	Flow chart – whom to sue	35
6.7	Particulars of claim – precedents	36
6.8	Defence – precedents	37
6.9	Expert witnesses	38
6.10	Claimant's checklist	39
6.11	Defendant's checklist	41
6.12	Limitation of actions	42
6.13	Legal Aid	42

7 Consumer Credit – Consumers — 43

7.1	Introduction	43
7.2	Consumers' questionnaire	43
7.3	Follow-up	45
7.4	Letters – the right style	45

8 Consumer Credit – Creditors — 47

8.1	Introduction	47
8.2	Creditors' questionnaire	47
8.3	Enforcement of the contract – procedure	49

8.4	Enforcement of the security – procedure	50
8.5	Recovery of the goods – procedure	50
8.6	Follow-up (subject to the client's instructions)	51

9 Consumer Credit – Common Problems   53

9.1	Applications by traders for licences	53
9.2	Credit reference agencies	55
9.3	Other incorrect information about consumers	56
9.4	Types of agreement – flow chart	57
9.5	Credit cards	59
9.6	The agreement – checklist	59

10 Consumer Credit – Litigation   61

10.1	Which court?	61
10.2	Checklist for creditor/owner-claimants	61
10.3	Particulars of claims relating to the delivery of goods to enforce an HP or conditional sale agreement	62
10.4	Particulars of claims relating to a time order	62
10.5	Precedent for consumers – claim arising out of the hirer's cancellation of agreement	63
10.6	Precedent for creditors – recovery of possession of goods, unpaid instalments and minimum sum under a contractual term	64
10.7	Precedent – a defence for consumers – a defect in the documents	66
10.8	Alternative to litigation	66

11 Unsolicited Goods and Services — 69

11.1   Introduction — 69

11.2   Procedure – unsolicited goods — 69

11.3   Offences – unsolicited goods — 70

11.4   Directories — 70

12 Consumer Safety – Defences for Suppliers — 71

12.1   Introduction — 71

12.2   Questionnaire – breach of general safety standard — 71

12.3   Follow-up — 73

12.4   Offences under the Consumer Protection Act 1987 — 73

12.5   Defences in respect of the general safety
requirement — 74

12.6   Penalties for offences in relation to the general
safety requirement — 76

12.7   Appeals procedure – prohibition notices — 76

12.8   Appeals procedure – notices to warn — 77

12.9   Appeals against suspension notices — 78

12.10 Forfeiture of goods – procedure — 78

12.11 Detention of goods – appeal procedure — 79

13 False Price Indications – Defences for Suppliers — 81

13.1   Introduction — 81

13.2   Questionnaire — 81

13.3   Follow-up — 82

13.4   Some points to watch out for — 82

13.5   Defences – the Consumer Protection Act 1987 — 84

14 Misleading Trade Descriptions – Defences for Suppliers   **87**

14.1   The offence in relation to goods   87

14.2   The offence in relation to services, accommodation
       or facilities   88

14.3   Questionnaire   88

14.4   Follow-up   88

14.5   Defences   89

15 Useful Names and Addresses   **91**

16 Further Reading   **97**

1 Basic Information

1.1 Consumers and suppliers

Although consumers need protection from the effects of defective products or unethical business practices, the customer is not always right. Anyone who works in customer relations' departments of the larger companies can tell true stories of how people have tried to cover up their own incompetence by making false claims that products are defective. Various statutes have recognised that suppliers need protection, too, by providing them with defences. This book is therefore written for suppliers, consumers and their respective advisers.

1.2 Definition of 'consumer'

Although, in general, a definition of 'consumer' could logically be related both to the status of the person buying the goods and services and the purpose for which they are to be used, in practice the various statutes have sometimes taken different approaches. For example, s 12(1) of the Unfair Contract Terms Act 1977 defines 'dealing as a consumer' by reference to three tests:

(a) the consumer neither makes the contract in the course of a business nor holds himself out as doing so; and

(b) the other party does make the contract in the course of a business; and

(c) in the case of the law of sale of goods or hire purchase or under s 7 of the Unfair Contract Terms Act 1977, the goods are of a type ordinarily supplied for private use or consumption.

However, s 12(2) excludes from this definition those who buy goods on a sale by auction or under a competitive tender.

The Consumer Credit Act 1974 defines a consumer credit agreement by reference, among other things, to an individual as a debtor (s 8(1)).

This means that sole traders and partnerships are consumers for the purposes of the Act.

For the purposes of the Unfair Terms in Consumer Contract Regulations 1999, 'a consumer' means 'any natural person who, in contracts covered by these Regulations, is acting for purposes which are outside his trade, business or profession' (reg 3.1) (para 2.1). This is derived from Art 2 of Council Directive (93/13/EC) of 15 April 1993, which adds 'trade' and 'profession' to 'business'.

It is therefore necessary to consider the relevant provisions of any of the statutes claiming to protect consumers to discover exactly who is being protected.

1.3 Sources – statutes

Laws relating to consumer protection are found in many statutes, of which the main ones are:

- Hire Purchase Act 1964;
- Consumer Credit Act 1974;
- Consumer Protection Act 1987;
- Factors Act 1889;
- Misrepresentation Act 1967;
- Road Traffic Act 1988;
- Sale of Goods Act 1979;
- Supply of Goods and Services Act 1982;
- Supply of Goods (Implied Terms) Act 1973;
- Torts (Interference with Goods) Act 1977;
- Trade Descriptions Act 1968;
- Unfair Contract Terms Act 1977;
- Food Standards Act 1999;
- Contracts (Rights of Third Parties) Act 1999.

1.4 Statutory instruments and the EU influence

One important European Union directive (1993/13/EC of 15 April 1993 – Unfair Terms in Consumer Contracts) is included in the Unfair Terms in Consumer Contracts Regulations 1999 SI 1999/2083.

There are also the Consumer Protection (Cancellation of Contracts Concluded away from Business) Regulations 1987 which enforce Council Directive (85/577/EC).

The Directive Consumer Protection for Distance Selling Contracts (97/7/EC of 20 May 2000) will result in regulations whereby businesses selling goods or services, for example, advertising with order forms, catalogues, by telephone or email, will have to reveal certain information about themselves and their products. This directive is a reminder that shopping via the Internet is growing and will introduce new legal problems.

2 Interviewing the Consumer-Client – Sale of Goods and Services

2.1 Introduction

When the consumer-client seeks advice, it is essential to obtain some preliminary information before any adviser goes into detail. The points at this stage which should be noted are:

(a) name and address of potential client;

(b) brief details of the nature of the problem;

(c) the amount likely to be claimed;

(d) objective of the potential client;

(e) whether or not legal aid is required.

The purpose of points (b) and (c) is to ascertain if there is a solution in law to the consumer's problem, or if it is economic to pursue a claim. It is, for example, not worth going to court over a defective £4.95 calculator, unless there is other damage.

That is why it is important to consider the objectives of the consumer (point (d)) who, in some instances, may want to pursue a small claim in order 'to teach them a lesson'. The interviewer will have to point out, before the courts do, under the Civil Practice Rules (CPR) (r 1(2)(c)), the costs of time, money and effort that might be involved. This aspect of the interview will, therefore, have to be steered by the interviewer, whose purpose will be merely to establish quickly whether or not there is a *prima facie* case to proceed further. The consumer must not at this point be allowed to go into the full story, which will have to be taken down later in the context of the detailed questionnaire. Because many problems will be small or not worth following up, this aspect of the client interview must be brief.

Once a case appears to be established, the question of cost must be faced. The interviewer must also find out whether or not the consumer is likely to require legal aid (point (e) above).

If a decision is made to go ahead, then the interviewer must question the consumer in more detail with the aid of the questionnaire.

2.2   Consumers' questionnaire

The right hand side of the questionnaire must contain a column for notes to assist in the follow-up. These will act as a reminder to obtain missing information (such as letters, faxes or emails from the supplier which the consumer has omitted to bring to the interview):

Client's name, date

Client's address

Brief summary of problem

Name and address of the supplier of the goods and services

Address of the supplier's registered office (if a company)

Date on which goods or services were ordered

Details of any advertising that may have induced the client to enter into the contract (NB: it may be necessary to check the supplier's website).

Details of any relevant promises made at the time of ordering the goods and services

Date or dates on which the goods or services were due to be supplied

Date or dates on which goods or services were supplied

Place at which the goods or services were, or were due to be, supplied

Details of any written agreement (including a contract governed by the Consumer Credit Act 1974)

Is the consumer being sued for payment and do they wish to counterclaim for the loss and damage out of the quality of the goods and services? YES/NO

Details of any receipts or written guarantees

Name and address of the hirer or granter of credit if the goods were supplied under a contract governed by the Consumer Credit Act 1974

Details of the goods or services supplied or ordered

Details of what went wrong

Details of any instruction book (if relevant)

Chronology of complaints made by customer (including names of representatives of the supplier, if known, as well as other bodies such as a trade association)

Details of correspondence with the supplier (if any) or other relevant people (for example, the hirer under an HP agreement)

Details of any damage or injury to property or to people as the result of the problem with the goods or services

Names and addresses of any injured persons other than the client

Names and addresses of any witnesses who may be relevant

Name and address of the supplier's liability insurers

Note of instructions from the client

Is the client covered by legal protection insurance? YES/NO

If YES, obtain the details

Legally aided? YES/NO

If YES, assist with completion of legal aid Green Form

If NO, obtain payment on account of costs

2.3 Completing the questionnaire

While the interviewer is completing the questionnaire the client should not, in general, be asked leading questions prompting the answer 'yes' or 'no'. These may lead to answers which are too specific and the client may then omit to mention important points. Many a case has been lost because, under cross examination, a further fact destroying a carefully prepared brief has been admitted.

For that reason, the final question should be something like 'What other relevant points do you have to tell me?'. This can often prompt the client to reveal other, perhaps essential, information. The interviewer will therefore not necessarily complete the form in the order that it is laid out, because the consumer will add to his or her story.

Whether or not the consumer is clear about the facts, he or she may be reticent when it comes to giving instructions. The reason is that client will expect the solicitor to give advice as to what to do, whereas the solicitor can be waiting for instructions from the client. This will happen even if the law and the various courses of action have been explained. That is why it is important to discover the client's motives from the outset, as mentioned in para 2.1 above.

2.4   Follow-up (subject to the client's instructions)

(a) Note time taken at interview and completion of questionnaire.

(b) Send a statement to the client for approval.

(c) Contact supplier (and creditor under a consumer credit agreement). At this stage a decision will have to be made as to whether or not this will be a formal letter before action (see para 2.5 below).

(d) Obtain missing information (for example, letters or receipts not supplied by the client at the interview).

(e) If the client is being sued under a consumer credit or similar agreement and wishes to counterclaim as a result of the poor quality of the goods or services received, serve a defence and counterclaim.

2.5   Letters – the right style

The first decision as to procedure will be whether or not a formal letter before action should be sent. This should only be done if the client has done everything possible to find a solution to the problem. The objective of the initial correspondence will be to obtain a remedy.

Large companies will receive many complaints – no one provides the perfect goods and services – so it is important to make the right points. Solicitors who deal with commercial people must use commercial techniques, and their letters must reflect these. Some rules help in this objective:

(a) Whenever possible, the letter should be addressed to someone. This will not always be possible where the big company supplying the allegedly defective goods and services has a large customer relations department. If the client does not have very much information, a telephone call to find out the details may be necessary, but all this costs money, so too much time must not be spent on this. In relation to companies, the letter could merely be addressed to the company secretary.

(b) When solutions are suggested, a useful technique is to offer alternatives, either of which are acceptable to the client. The reason for this is that the reader of the letter will hopefully be deciding which of the two is the best for his or her business, so that the third option of not making a decision at all does not arise.

(c) The supplier must be informed of the benefits of settling the dispute – salespeople call this technique 'selling the benefits' rather than the product itself.

2.6   Precedent letter to seller

A letter to a large supplier of electrical goods

The Customer Relations Department
Unsound Goods Company Limited
Eastcheap
London

Dear Sirs

Re: Your Midi Stereo System and our Client Mr John Smith

We are instructed by Mr John Smith regarding his purchase of the — Stereo System at your Cheapside Branch on Saturday, 12 December 20—, for which he paid £1,000 as recorded on your receipt number 111111, but the following additional facts require your attention.

They arise out of his action at home that evening when he set the equipment up in accordance with the instruction book supplied with it. The sound quality was very poor, and much to his horror and amazement the auto-stop not only failed to work, but the tape broke in the machine. He therefore ran a blank tape through the machine to test this facility and it, too, was broken. He then became alarmed at the smell of burning from the Stereo System, and the plug then fused.

He sought help from your company but the telephone lines to the branch were constantly engaged and it was not until the following Wednesday that Mr Smith was able to speak to anyone. He does not know the name of the person he spoke to, but he did ask for the manager, and he was told the shop was too busy with the Christmas rush to deal with queries relating to defective equipment. Since then, Mr Smith has written to the branch but has had no reply. He subsequently telephoned your customer service department, but he got no further than recorded messages and music.

This is most unsatisfactory, but in these circumstances one of the following alternatives obviously provides you with a solution to the problem:

(1) on the return of the Stereo System to refund a total of £1,050 which includes the cost of replacing the tapes and a contribution towards his costs in pursuing the matter; or

(2) to replace the equipment free of charge and to give him a credit note for £50 redeemable at any of your branches. Mr Smith has never had any such problems with your staff before, so this will enable your company to retain some goodwill and a customer. We are sure you will agree that either of these are good solutions to the difficulty.

We therefore look forward to hearing which of the solutions are acceptable to you. However, if you do not respond to this letter by Friday 20 January 20—, we are instructed to start legal proceedings against your company.

3 Interviewing the Seller-Client – Sale of Goods and Services

3.1 Introduction

When the supplier of goods or services comes for advice about consumer problems, it is usually because a court action has already commenced. If a letter before action only has been received, then, where the situation calls for a compromise or for none, there may be time to prevent matters from going further. The supplier, in any event, will often be consulting a solicitor because he or she feels, sometimes rightly, that the consumer is being unreasonable or wrong.

In order to find out whether or not this is true, it is essential to obtain some preliminary information. The points at this stage which should be noted are:

(a) name, address and telephone number of the potential client;

(b) brief details of the nature of the problem;

(c) amount likely to be claimed;

(d) any relevant insurance policies (for example, legal protection or product liability);

(e) is legal aid required? – this does not, of course, apply to companies, but a sole trader may need it.

Not all clients accused of, for example, a breach of contract in relation to goods, will be the actual supplier. This arises out of s 75 of the Consumer Credit Act 1974 which, for example, makes a creditor liable for breach of contract relating to the quality of the goods provided by the supplier.

The purpose is to discover whether there is a *prima facie* defence to any allegations, or whether the supplier should surrender or try to find a compromise. If the supplier wishes to be represented by a lawyer, then the detailed suppliers' questionnaire can be completed.

In this context, some of the points made in Chapter 2 (para 2.1) are also relevant.

3.2 Suppliers' questionnaire

(NB: as with the consumers' questionnaire, the right hand column of the questionnaire must contain a column for notes to assist in the follow-up.)

Client's name, date

Client's address and telephone number

Name of contacts at the client's business

Brief summary of the problem

If the problem relates to goods, the name and address of the supplier and date on which they were supplied

Details of any contract with that supplier

If the problem relates to services which in the event were provided by a sub-contractor, the name and address of that sub-contractor

Details of any contract with that sub-contractor

Date or dates on which the goods and services were ordered

Date or dates on which the goods and services were supplied

Place at which the goods or services were, or were to be, supplied

Details of any written agreement (including a contract governed by the Consumer Credit Act 1974)

Details of any instruction book (if relevant)

Chronology of any correspondence with the consumer

Details of any correspondence with third parties (for example, trade associations)

Details of any damage or injury to people or property as a result of the alleged problem with the goods or services

Names and addresses of the client's employees who have had dealings with the consumer

Details of any other problems with the same goods or services (for example, number and type of complaints)

Names and addresses of any other witnesses

Names and addresses of the supplier's liability insurers and details of any relevant insurance policy

Note of instructions from the client

Legally aided (sole traders only)? YES/NO

If YES, assist with the completion of legal aid Green Form

If NO, obtain payment on account of costs

3.3   Follow-up (subject to the client's instructions)

(a) Note time taken at interview and completion of questionnaire.

(b) Send a statement to the client for approval.

(c) If relevant, prepare a defence (see Chapter 6).

(d) If responsibility can be passed to another supplier or sub-contractor write letters to them. Note the comments on style and content of such letters as mentioned in Chapter 2 (paras 2.5 and 2.6)

(e) If relevant, contact the liability insurers and obviously check that they are happy with your firm's involvement.

(f) Reply to correspondence and inform either the consumer, or those solicitors representing him or her, that the supplier has appointed solicitors. If the case is weak or a compromise will save everyone a lot of time and money, then a solution to the dispute should be suggested.

4 Common Problems in Contract

4.1 Formation of the contract

Questions relating to the existence or otherwise of a consumer contract usually arise out of the informal nature of the arrangements. The answers are found by taking the facts as noted on the relevant questionnaires and applying the basic principles to them, that is:

(a) an offer followed by;

(b) acceptance (which may be by conduct (*Thornton v Shoe Lane Parking Ltd* [1971] 2 QB 163));

(c) certainty in the contractual terms;

(d) consideration;

(e) an intention to create legal relations;

(f) for a lawful purpose;

(g) an agreement between persons with the capacity to make a contract.

Electronics have changed some of the ways that consumers buy goods and services, although the basic principles still apply.

In the case of EftPos (Electronic Funds Transfer at the Point of Sale), people may pay for goods and services through, for example, the Switch system, by means of their plastic cards. Funds are transferred electronically from a consumer's bank account into that of the supplier.

People, however, do not have to go out to shop, in that they may place orders by sending a fax, email, or by logging onto a supplier's website. In those circumstances, a contract will be concluded instantaneously in accordance with the principles in *Entores v Miles Far East Corp* [1955] 2 QB 327. Electronic equipment can, unfortunately, break down, so this must be considered in the light of the principle that acceptance must be communicated to the other side. This may be difficult to prove.

This electronic means of communication can cause another difficulty, in that, through the internet, consumers can easily buy goods from other countries, particularly in the European Union. Not only does that raise the question of which law governs the contract, but there is also the problem of seeking a remedy from a supplier in a different jurisdiction. The Civil Jurisdiction and Judgments Act 1982 allows a consumer the choice of an action in his or her own country of domicile or in the country where the other party is domiciled, provided that the latter's country is a Contracting State (Sched 1, Art 14).

4.2   Misrepresentation

A common problem in consumer transactions arises out of what the salesperson has said and whether or not it is material. The following points must be considered:

(a) The representation must have been unambiguous (*New Brunswick & Canada Rly v Muggeridge* [1860] 1 Dr & Sm 363) and must have induced the consumer to have entered into the contract (*Traill v Baring* [1864] 4 DJ & S 318).

(b) There is no cause of action if it was ignored by the consumer (*Smith v Chadwick* [1884] 9 App Cas 187).

(c) A contract will, however, sometimes try to exclude antecedent negotiations, but this may be defeated by the Unfair Contract Terms Act 1977.

(d) Rescission of the contract in relation to innocent misrepresentation may be possible as a result of the terms of the Misrepresentation Act 1967.

Lawyers representing either consumers or businesses must, therefore, question their clients or potential clients very carefully, because people may interpret, rather than remember, what happened. Vague responses must be probed further, because it is no use to pursue a lost cause.

4.3   Advertising

In addition to the points mentioned in para 4.2 above, misleading advertising can lead to criminal convictions under such as the Trade Descriptions Act 1968 and the Consumer Transactions (Restrictions on Statements) Order 1976 SI 1976/1813. In this respect, a supplier may have been advertising on a website and, unless the consumer has printed out the advertisement, it may be difficult to prove that a particular inducement was made by that means.

It may be worth investigating whether or not the retailer has been convicted as a result of the facts related by the consumer. Such a conviction could be useful evidence (see s 11 of the Civil Evidence Act 1968). Local trading standards officers may assist with this information. Complaints can also be made to the Advertising Standards Authority, whose address is noted in Chapter 15.

4.4 Deposits and prepayments

Consumers often have problems with deposits which they have paid, if they subsequently find that they do not want the goods or services offered. If the money paid is effectively a guarantee that the contract will be performed, then it is a deposit which may not be returned unless otherwise agreed if the consumer decides not to go ahead with the transaction (*Howe v Smith* [1884] 27 CD 89).

Where the sum paid is substantial, the court may follow the decision in *Dies v British & International Mining & Finance Co Ltd* [1939] 1 KB 724. In that case, there was no mention of the word 'deposit' in the contract so, in the absence of this and subject to any claim of the seller in damages, the money had to be returned.

What is substantial may be difficult to judge and appeals may have to be made to the erstwhile seller's better nature.

4.5 Ownership

Questions of title often arise in the sale of used cars. One aspect is mistaken identity, but others arise out of s 12 of the Sale of Goods Act 1979 (or ss 2 or 7 of the Supply of Goods and Services Act 1982 or s 8 of the Supply of Goods (Implied Terms) Act 1973). The effect of the decision in *Butterworth v Kingsway Motors Ltd* [1954] 1 WLR 1286 is well known, but other aspects of ownership can arise out of s 25(1) of that Act and s 9 of the Factors Act 1889.

In these circumstances, an innocent purchaser may be allowed to keep what were originally stolen goods, although often such a buyer may not be disputing ownership with the original owner but with a big and powerful insurance company (see *National Employers' Mutual General Insurance Association Ltd v Jones* [1987] 3 WLR 901, affirmed by the House of Lords ([1988] 2 WLR 952)). This practical aspect must colour any advice given to clients.

4.6   Quality

Most consumer problems probably arise out of the quality of the goods and the answers in law are to be found in the cases arising out of, as well as the actual wording of:

(a) ss 12–15 of the Sale of Goods Act 1979;

(b) ss 3–5 and ss 8–10 of the Supply of Goods and Services Act 1982;

(c) ss 9–11 of the Supply of Goods (Implied Terms) Act 1973.

Note, however, that goods have to be of satisfactory quality (s 14 of the Sale of Goods Act 1979 and s 4 of the Supply of Goods and Services Act 1982). Although the test of fitness for purpose remains, there are others, including appearance and finish, freedom from minor defects, safety and durability.

Sometimes, a supplier is moved to dispute a consumer's claim merely because no opportunity has been given to examine the goods to find out whether they are really defective. Where the supplier is a reputable one, this gives the opening for the lawyer to negotiate a settlement.

Questions of quality may have to be answered by experts, and the cost of these may have to be measured against the value of the claim and the possible risk of losing the action. Sound advice must be given to consumers in these circumstances and they must be carefully questioned to find out whether or not they really want to proceed at all costs.

4.7   Avoiding liability

Suppliers of goods and services will sometimes seek to avoid liability by pointing out some exclusion clause, although the provisions of the Unfair Contract Terms Act 1977 (for example, s 6(2)) and the Unfair Terms in Consumer Contracts Regulations 1994 SI 1994/3159 will usually be sufficient to stop such arguments.

It is, however, important to note that the onus of proof that there was a consumer sale lies on the person making such an assertion. In *Rasboro Ltd v JCL Marine Ltd* [1977] 1 Lloyds Rep 645, a yacht was ostensibly purchased by a company in Jersey, although all the parties knew that the real purchaser was to be the owner of the business. When the yacht sank, the sellers' exclusion clause did not apply and they had to pay damages.

There is a potential problem in relation to goods of a type ordinarily supplied for private use or consumption. For example, a home computer sold primarily for its games programs will cause no difficulty, but some computers are modestly priced and used by both businesses and private individuals, although they have both word processing and games programs. The question is more difficult when a consumer buys what is primarily a business micro computer for home use, because it may not be really of a type supplied for that purpose. If something goes wrong, a consumer may have to hope that the courts will take a broad view of the provision.

4.8 Consumer credit

The questionnaire in relation to the supply of goods (para 3.2) should be used when a hirer, etc, under a consumer credit agreement comes for advice in relation to a problem arising out of those goods themselves. For example, questions as to the legal liability of the quality, or lack of it, in relation to the goods may be answered by ss 9–11 of the Supply of Goods (Implied Terms) Act 1973, which are similar to those in ss 13–15 of the Sale of Goods Act 1979.

4.9 Time

Consumers often will have heard that time is of the essence in a contract, but sometimes they will have to be educated that time has to be made the essence. A supplier who has not been informed of the consumer's urgent need for the goods or services, may have a defence to an action based on late performance.

4.10 Delivery and acceptance

Acceptance of the goods can reduce a claim for recision of contract under ss 13–15 of the Sale of Goods Act 1979 into one for damages. Although the shopkeeper rightly wants to be assured that the customer has not misused his or her purchase, once it is in the hands of a repairer, the purchaser may be persuaded reluctantly to accept a repair rather than a refund or replacement goods. Since 3 January 1995, an agreement or request by a buyer for a repair does not infer acceptance. Furthermore, although the rule of privity of contract remains, a 'sub-sale or other disposition' (such as a gift) is also not deemed to be an acceptance. A person who has given a present (but not the donee) may still be able to claim recision of contract in respect of a defective product.

4.11 Instruction books

Although the plaintiff lost his case in *Wormell v RHM Agriculture (East) Ltd* [1987] 1 WLR 1091, the general principle that instruction books formed part of the contract of sale was approved. This is logical in the light of the provision in relation to reliance on the seller in s 14 of the Sale of Goods Act 1979.

Questions as to the understanding, or lack of it, of the consumer can arise in these circumstances. Advisers of consumers should have no problems where an instruction book is wrong or seems to be a direct translation from the Japanese, so that the goods are used wrongly and are damaged.

There could, however, be more difficulty if the instruction book is fairly clear but the consumer is of limited intelligence. There is no particular guidance on this through the cases, but save that if the instructions are at least ambiguous, there is a possible breach of contract (the *Wormell* case).

4.12 Gifts and privity

People give presents, but the recipient of a defective article has to overcome the doctrine of privity of contract in order to obtain redress. The Contracts (Rights of Third Parties) Act 1999 allows a third party to enforce a contractual term provided that the contract expressly provides for it and that it identifies that party in some way (s 1). This will limit its usefulness.

Another method by which they can obtain a remedy is by means of s 5 of the Unfair Contract Terms Act 1977. It applies to anyone other than the party to the contract under which possession or ownership of the goods passed, if the goods have been found to be defective while in consumer use, and the defect resulted from the negligence of the manufacturer or distributor. Consumer use arises out of a purpose 'otherwise than exclusively for the purposes of a business'. This section is obviously more concerned with tort, which is described more fully in the following chapter.

It may be possible to imply a collateral contract to the main agreement, which will protect strangers to the latter. In *Shanklin Pier Ltd v Dettel Products Ltd* [1951] 2 All ER 471, the suppliers of paint warranted by them to be suitable were liable to the pier company, whose contractors had actually bought the paint.

Advisers of consumers who have been given defective goods will more usually bring a claim in tort and merely allege that a collateral contract existed so as to cover all eventualities.

Another way to solve the problem is for the purchaser who gave the present to sue on the original contract (see para 4.10 above).

4.13 Guarantees

Retailers often use guarantees as selling aids, so under Art 4 of the Consumer Transactions (Restrictions on Statements) Order 1976 SI 1976/1813, such a guarantee must state that it is in addition to any rights a consumer may have. It must not, furthermore, take such rights away.

This does not prevent retailers from stating that they will replace or repair defective goods, provided that they also include a statement that this is in addition to the other rights of the consumer. If a problem with the goods arises, the shopkeeper may be tempted to point to the specific promise in the guarantee and insist on sending the defective product away for repair. The consumer, not aware that he or she, for example, in certain circumstances could obtain a full refund of the purchase price, may feel forced to accept the retailer's offer.

This problem is overcome by s 5 of the Unfair Contract Terms Act 1977, which forbids the exclusion or restriction of compensation for loss or damage by means of a guarantee in respect of consumer goods. The meaning of such goods is tested by reference to their actual use by the purchaser. A written guarantee is defined as a promise or assurance 'that defects will be made good by complete or partial replacement, or by repair, monetary compensation or otherwise'.

There are, further, the Unfair Terms in Consumer Contract Regulations 1999 SI 1999/2083, whereby a seller cannot transfer the consumer's rights and obligation so as to reduce his or her guarantees (para 1(p) of Sched 2).

4.14 Limitation of liability

Section 2(1) of the Unfair Contract Terms Act 1977 prohibits contractual terms which purport to exclude or restrict liability for death or personal injury resulting from negligence. Sub-section (2) applies the reasonableness test to any other terms restricting liability for negligence, although a consumer's awareness of any such clause is not evidence that he or she has accepted the risk (sub-s (3)).

Suppliers of goods and services will often provide standard printed contracts, and then will try and avoid liability by reference to one of its terms. By s 3 of the Unfair Contract Terms Act 1977, any term in a written standard terms contract which purports to restrict or exclude liability for breach or which permits performance in a substantially different form is subject to the reasonableness test.

Of greater importance are the Unfair Terms in Consumer Contracts Regulations 1999 SI 1999/2083, which govern standard contracts drafted in advance and where the consumer has not been able to influence the substance of the term (para 5(2)). An unfair term is one 'which contrary to the requirement of good faith causes a significant imbalance in the parties' rights and obligations arising under the contract to the detriment of the consumer'. An indication of particular unfair terms is set out in Sched 3 to the Regulations and specific problems arising out of such contracts are noted in para 4.15 below.

Another way of overcoming this problem is by reference to s 11, where a contract term is to be fair and reasonable 'having regard to the circumstances which were, or ought reasonably to have been, known to or in the contemplation of the parties when the contract was made'. The burden of proof is on the person claiming the term to be reasonable. Note, in particular, *Woodman v Photo Trade Processing Ltd* [1981] NLJ 131, where a term limited liability to the film if the processor should be in breach of a contract for developing and printing. This was held to be unreasonable in relation to lost wedding photographs, but it is possible that it would have been reasonable had the company offered an alternative higher-quality service covered by, say, insurance against loss.

Another means of restricting liability occurs where customers have to look at notices or other documents containing exclusion clauses. The famous ticket cases such as *Chappleton v Barry Urban District Council* [1940] 1 KB 532 are helpful to consumers in this context. Similar considerations apply to a course of dealing (*McCutcheon v David MacBrayne Ltd* [1964] 1 All ER 430). In *Interfoto Picture Library Ltd v Stiletto Visual Programmes Ltd* [1989] QB 433, it was held that, where printed conditions in a contract were particularly onerous, the party enforcing them had to show they had been sufficiently brought to the attention of the other.

4.15 Particular problems with standard form contracts

Sellers can less easily evade responsibility for defective products as a result of the Unfair Terms in Consumer Contracts Regulations 1999 SI 1999/2083, as noted in para 4.13 above, but there are two problem areas. These arise from Sched 2 to the Regulations, which includes examples of unfair terms such as:

(a) a term 'enabling the seller or supplier to alter unilaterally without valid reason any characteristics of the product or service to be provided' (para 1(k), Sched 2); and

(b) in certain circumstances, a term providing for the price to be determined at the time of delivery (para 11(1), Sched 2).

Advertisements or contracts sometimes reserve the right of the seller to change specifications. In some instances, say where goods have to be supplied and fitted at a later date. The supplier reserves the right to change prices, perhaps because of increases in the cost of materials or labour.

4.16 Holidays

In addition to points arising out of misrepresentation, there are two important points to remember when clients complain that their holiday has not lived up to the expectations promised by the brochure:

(a) there may be damages for themselves and their families arising out of loss of enjoyment, as noted in the next paragraph (and, also, see *Jarvis v Swan Tours* [1973] 1 QB 233, as well as *Jackson v Horizon Holidays* [1975] 1 WLR 1468); and

(b) the Association of British Travel Agents has an arbitration scheme (see para 6.2).

4.17 Loss of enjoyment, generally

In considering any consumer problem, advisers must remember that the remedy arising out of loss of enjoyment is no longer restricted to holidays. In *Woodman v Photo Trade Processing Ltd* [1981] NLJ 131, the plaintiff recovered £75 in a claim arising out of the loss of wedding photographs by the film processor.

5 Common Problems in Tort

5.1 Negligence

Negligence, in fact, provides an answer to some common consumer problems, as follows:

(a) The defective goods are a gift, so there is no contractual relationship between the consumer, who has suffered the loss and damage, and the seller.

(b) The seller has gone out of business and there is no contractual relationship between the business, which manufactured the defective goods causing the loss and damage, and the consumer.

(c) The main contractor has gone out of business, but the loss and damage was caused by an existing sub-contractor with whom the consumer had no contractual relationship.

(d) The manufacturer of the goods has gone out of business, but the loss and damage were caused by a defective component provided by an existing sub-contractor with whom the injured consumer would obviously have had no contractual relationship.

(e) The manufacturer of the goods has gone out of business, but the loss and damage arose out of a faulty design by a sub-contractor.

In any event, negligence can often be pleaded, as well, when the cause of action arises out of breach of contract. A manufacturer (or its insurance company) will also pass the blame onto sub-contractors and join them as a party to the action. Solicitors advising clients accused of supplying defective goods and services to consumers must explore this line of defence.

Although it may be possible to claim *res ipsa loquitur*, the elements of negligence (that is, a breach of a duty of care owed to the claimant followed by reasonably foreseeable loss and damage) have to be proved.

An additional cause of action may be available under the Consumer Protection Act 1987 mentioned in more detail in para 5.4 below. Evidence that the product was defective and the cause of the damage only is needed.

5.2   Product recall

Sometimes, a complaint by a consumer can highlight that others of the same product are defective. If there is a risk that the defect will result in death, injury, damage to property, or economic loss, then the distributor or manufacturer must be persuaded to recall the offending product.

Although the Consumer Protection Act 1987 gives enforcement authorities considerable powers, for example, to prohibit the sale of potentially unsafe goods and to publish information about them (s 13), there are no provisions about product recall procedure as such. Willis J in *Walton v British Leyland (UK) Ltd* (1978) 12 June, QBD said that, in that case, the defendant had a duty of care to the public to make a clean breast of the problem, and recall all the potentially defective products it could for safety washers to be fitted. The distributor or manufacturer should take the initiative, so it can control the product recall procedure, which may be an expensive, but obviously essential exercise, as will be the resulting publicity.

The procedure will depend on what records are available on the ownership of the goods. In the case of vehicles, the Vehicle Licensing Office in Swansea will provide useful information, while in other cases the distributor or manufacturer will have detailed records. In most cases this will not be possible, so advertisements and press releases will be needed.

Although lawyers consulted by such distributors and manufacturers will not be expected to give other than legal advice in these circumstances, some general points must be brought to the client's attention:

(a) The product recall campaign should be co-ordinated perhaps by means of a committee of appropriately qualified executives and with the full backing of the company decision makers.

(b) The campaign will usually require a combination of technical and marketing expertise – the latter in particular may have to handle the effects of the possible poor publicity on business operations.

Even if product recall is not necessary in the particular instance, a distributor or manufacturer may well be advised to take out insurance cover for that risk.

5.3 Economic loss

Damages for economic loss in tort create particular problems and the position, in addition to the requirements as to foreseeability (see *Aswan Engineering Co M/S v Lupdine Ltd* [1987] 1 WLR 1), can be summarised thus:

(a) they will only be granted where there is a very close proximity akin to a contractual relationship between the parties (see *Junior Books v Veitchi* [1982] 3 All ER 201 in the light of *D & F Estates Ltd v Church Commissioners* [1989] AC 177);

(b) otherwise, they will only be payable to a consumer by his or her immediate vendor (see *Muirhead v Industrial Tank Specialities* [1985] 3 WLR 993);

(c) but negligence plus reasonable foreseeability of the loss which occurred, are not by themselves sufficient to establish a cause of action (see, generally, *Murphy v Brentwood District Council* [1991] 1 AC 398, HL).

Liability under the Consumer Protection Act 1987 is similarly restricted to death, personal injury and loss or damage to property (s 5).

The effect of these authorities is that damages for economic loss caused by third parties will only be recovered in very limited circumstances, so clients must be warned of the risks of litigation in such cases.

5.4 Product liability under the Consumer Protection Act 1987

Some consumers who have received defective goods as a present or who have bought them from a retailer now out of business, obviously have no contractual remedy. They may sometimes be able to turn to the Consumer Protection Act 1987, which makes other people responsible for defective products as follows:

(a) the producer of the products;

(b) importers of the products into the EC;

(c) those distributors who mark the product with their own trade marks (but, note that many such businesses are planning to add what are effectively disclaimers that the trade mark does not mean that they have produced the goods);

(d) those retailers or producers who do not respond to a request to information about the true identity of the supplier of the products to them.

The remedies available to consumers arise out of the supplier's or importer's breach of statutory duty.

Furthermore, according to s 1, 'product' has a wide definition, while 'defect' is defined by reference to safety (s 3). It is necessary to prove that a defective product caused death, personal injury or damage to property. Note, however, that it does not apply to small claims under £275 (s 5) where consumers will have to rely on other remedies in contract or in tort.

Duties are defined further in the General Product Safety Regulations 1994 SI 1994/2328. Producers must place safe products on the market (r 7) and distributors must use due care to help ensure compliance with that duty (r 9). There is a general presumption that a product complies with UK health and safety requirements unless the contrary is proved (r 10(1)) – an important evidential point.

The Consumer Protection Act 1987 is not a solution to all problems, and the types of defence available will also have to be considered (para 5.5 below) before any action can be taken.

5.5   Defences under the Consumer Protection Act 1987

Solicitors advising businesses blamed by consumers for loss or damage under the Consumer Protection Act 1987 must consider the defences:

(a) They complied with a statutory or Community obligation, that is, the Act is concerned with minimum standards (s 4(1)(a)) and see, also, the General Product Safety Regulations mentioned in 5.4 above (r 10).

(b) They did not supply the goods (s 4(1)(b)).

(c) The goods were supplied other than in the course of a business or for a profit (s 4(1)(c)).

(d) The defect did not exist at the relevant time as defined by sub-s (2) (s 4(1)(d)).

(e) The state of the art at the relevant time was such that the defect could not have been discovered (s 4(1)(e)).

(f) The defect was due to another, that is, the designer or, alternatively, the product was made exactly in accordance with the instructions of another, the true producer.

(g) The product is not of a type ordinarily intended for private use and was not intended to be used as such by the consumer – in some instances this may be a cause of much argument (s 5(2)).

(h) The damage was less than £275 (s 5(4)).

(i) The case is brought out of time (this topic is dealt with in more detail in para 6.12).

5.6 Detention of goods

People sometimes have problems when they lend their property to someone else or send them to a repairer, but then find it difficult to get it back again. Most of the answers to this problem are found in the Torts (Interference with Goods) Act (T(IwG)A) 1977. Section 2(2) allows an action for the loss or destruction of goods which a bailee has allowed to happen in breach of his duty to the bailor.

If the goods are wrongfully detained (s 3(2)), a court can grant one of the following remedies:

(a) It may make an order for the delivery of the goods and for payment of any consequential damage. This remedy is only granted at the discretion of the court (s 3(3)(b) of the T(IwG)A), but if the bailee does not comply with it, the order may be revoked in whole or in part and damages may be awarded instead (s 3(4) of the T(IwG)A).

(b) An order may be made for the delivery of the goods, but the bailee has the alternative of paying damages by reference to the value of the goods. In either event, the bailee may also have to pay any consequential damages. If the bailee satisfies the order by returning the goods before execution of judgment, it is without prejudice to any liability to pay any consequential damages (s 3(5) of the T(IwG)A).

(c) The court may simply award damages to the bailor, which will result in the extinction of the bailor's title to the goods (s 5 of the T(IwG)A).

Where goods are returned, an allowance may have to be made for any improvement to the goods (ss 3(6), (7) and 6 of the T(IwG)A). Where there is more than one claimant to the goods, the wrongdoer does not have a double liability (s 7 of the T(IwG)A).

Although co-ownership is no defence if, for example, one of the owners has destroyed the property (s 10 of the T(IwG)A), it is a defence that a third party has a better right than that of the claimant (s 8 of the T(IwG)A. Where one of two or more co-owners wishes to bring an action on behalf of the other or others, the particulars of claim must identify all such persons (CCR Ord 15, r 4(1)). If a defendant wishes to show that a third party has a better right to the goods, notice of the application must be served on that party. If he or she fails to appear or comply with a court order, an order may be made by the court to deprive him or her of any right in the action (CCR Ord 15, r 4(3)).

In an emergency, interlocutory relief is possible under s 4 (T(IwG)A) (and see, also, Rules of the Supreme Court Ord 29, r 2A as well as CCR Ord 13, r 7(1)(d) and (2)).

5.7   Uncollected goods

Repairers and cleaners often are left with goods they have repaired or cleaned, but the customer never comes back to collect them. The T(IwG)A 1977 provides two solutions, which may be combined in certain circumstances. The bailee must, however, be in the situation envisaged by s 12(1), that is, in possession or in control of the goods, where:

(a) the bailor is in breach of his or her obligation to collect, or to give directions in respect of the delivery of, the goods;

(b) the bailee could impose such obligations but the bailor cannot be contacted or be traced;

(c) the bailee could reasonably expect to be relieved of any duty to safeguard the goods on giving notice to the bailor, but the latter can similarly not be contacted or traced.

The first remedy is contained in Pt II of the Schedule to the T(IwG)A 1977, which allows the bailee to impose an obligation to collect the goods subject to notice. This notice in writing given either to the bailor, left at his or her proper address (T(IwG)A, Sched 1, Pt I, para 1(2)) must contain the following information (T(IwG)A, Sched 1, Pt I, para 1(3)):

(a) the name and address of the bailee, sufficient particulars of the goods and the address or place at which they are held;

(b) a statement that the goods are ready for delivery to the bailor, or when they will be ready if this is combined with a notice terminating the contract of bailment (note that the notice may be given at any time after the goods have been repaired, treated or appraised under the contract of bailment (T(IwG)A, Sched 1, Pt I, paras 2 and 3) while custodians other than mercantile agents may give notice in a similar manner (T(IwG)A, Sched 1, Pt I, para 4));

(c) a statement of any amounts payable by the bailor in respect of the goods and which were due before the giving of notice.

If notice is served by registered post or recorded delivery (T(IwG)A, Sched 1, Pt II, para 6(4)), it may be combined with a notice of intention to sell under Pt II of the Act. It must contain the following information (T(IwG)A, Sched 1, Pt II, para 6(1)):

(a) the name and address of the bailee, sufficient particulars of the goods and the address or place at which they are held;

(b) the date on or after which the bailee proposes to sell the goods;

(c) a statement of any amounts payable by the bailor in respect of the goods and which were due before the giving of notice, in which case the period of notice must be not less than three months (T(IwG)A, Sched 1, Pt II, para 6(3)).

Such a notice may not be served if there is a dispute concerning the goods unless the court has made an order under s 13 of the T(IwG)A. Under that provision, the court must be satisfied that the bailee is entitled to sell under s 12 and had given notice in accordance with the provisions of Sched 1.

The entitlement to sell can only be exercised if notice has been given under Pt II of Sched 1, or the bailee has failed to trace or communicate with the bailor with a view to giving such notice after having taken reasonable steps for that purpose (s 12(3)(b) of the T(IwG)A). As far as companies are concerned, notice must be served on the registered or principal office, but in the case of individuals the last known address will suffice (T(IwG)A, Sched 1, Pt II, para 8). The bailee must also be reasonably satisfied that the bailor owns the goods (s 12(3)(b) of the T(IwG)A).

There are some potential problems arising out of the sale of the goods in these circumstances, but s 12(4) of the T(IwG)A responds that where the bailor was not the owner, a sale shall not give good title against the latter. It is, however, good title against the bailor (s 12(6) of the T(IwG)A).

A bailee is also liable to account for the sale less costs of sale, and any sum payable to him or her by the bailor before the notice of intention was served (s 12(5) of the T(IwG)A). The bailee also has the duty of adopting the best method of sale in the circumstances.

5.8 Advising suppliers on their own procedures

A claim by a consumer may reveal deficiencies in the administrative systems of the supplier of allegedly defective goods. If products are causing problems, then it is important that the relevant distributor and manufacturer know about these at an early stage, and that they react quickly. Proper procedures will help both to avoid consumer claims and to provide vital evidence if needed. If they do not have the proper procedures, businesses supplying consumer goods should be advised to mend their ways.

6 Litigation – Sale of Goods and Services

6.1 Introduction

In many instances, the intervention of a solicitor will result in a solution to the problem and either the supplier will accept a *without prejudice* settlement or there will be a compromise. In other cases, litigation will be needed.

6.2 Alternatives to courts

Before any action is taken through the courts, other means of obtaining a remedy should be considered. These arise out of arbitration schemes run by trade associations such as the Association of British Travel Agents (ABTA) and the Motor Agents Association. They are appropriate where:

(a) the claim is a small one (for example, the ABTA arbitration scheme covers claims up to £1,500 per person and up to £7,500 per booking);

(b) the supplier is a member of the relevant trade association;

(c) the dispute does not involve points of law (for example, the ABTA arbitration scheme does not cover claims arising solely or mainly in respect of physical injury or illness or their consequences);

(d) the supplier in disputing the facts as presented by the consumer has otherwise been co-operative.

Where it seems as though this procedure may be appropriate, the following measures should be taken:

(a) Consider whether or not the claim is disputed largely on the facts.

(b) If it is, check whether or not the supplier is a member of a trade association – this will be indicated on its letterhead.

(c) If it is a member of such an association, write to that body and obtain the details of any arbitration procedure and of any relevant codes of practice (for example, ABTA has both a Tour Operators' Code of Conduct and a Travel Agents' Code of Conduct).

(d) Once the details have been received, check to see whether or not the arbitration rules are appropriate to resolving the dispute.

(e) If they are, then take action in accordance with those rules, but otherwise commence litigation.

6.3   Contractual arbitration clauses

The Arbitration Act 1996 extends the application of the Unfair Terms in Consumer Contracts Regulations 1999 SI 1999/2083, in that any term forcing a consumer to go to arbitration where the claim is below £5,000 is deemed to be unfair.

6.4   Alternative dispute resolution

The Civil Procedure Rules encourage the parties to use alternative dispute resolution (ADR) (CPR 1.4(2)(e)) to settle the case either in whole or in part (CPR 1.4(2)(f)). If the possibility of such mediation has not arisen earlier, it may well be a factor in the allocation questionnaire. This is an opportunity for either, or both, of the parties to state whether they would like the action to be stayed for a month to allow ADR or a settlement generally. Note the wide case management powers of the court (CPR 3) which include the making of any steps or order 'for the purpose of managing the case and furthering the overall objective' (CPR 3.2(m)). Many consumer disputes concern facts rather than a detailed interpretation of the law, so mediation or arbitration should always be considered.

6.5   Which court?

Small claims track – this is the normal track where the claim is not more than £5,000 (CPR 26.6(3)), but the figure is reduced to £1,000 in respect of a claim for personal injuries (CPR 26.6(1)(a)(ii)). Otherwise, the claim must be very straightforward (Practice Direction supplementing CPR 26). Many consumer problems will be small, so will fall into this category, but only fixed costs will be awarded to a successful party. Those people who insist on representation must be informed of this rule, before they set out on litigation.

The County Court deals with claims of less than £15,000, or in the case of personal injury the figure is £50,000. The High Court will deal with larger matters.

The fast track is deemed to be suitable for most defended claims between £5,000 and £15,000 and a trial anticipated to last for not more than a day.

6.6   Flow chart – whom to sue

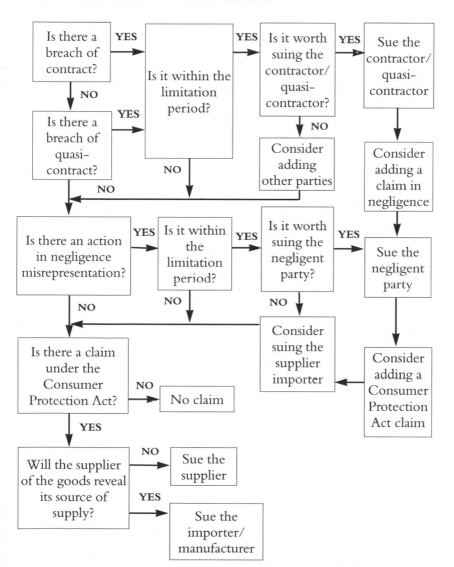

6.7   Particulars of claim – precedents

6.7.1 Sale of goods

Particulars of claim

(a) At all material times the defendant was a retailer of electronic and electrical equipment.

(b) By an oral agreement made on 1 July 20__ in the defendant's shop at 1 High Street, Glastontown, Wessex, the defendant by a shop assistant agreed to sell to the claimant an XYZ midi system bearing his trade mark at a price of £1,050.

(c) The defendant sold the said midi system in the course of business for the private use of the claimant. In the premises it was an implied condition that the goods would be of merchantable quality.

(d) In breach of the said condition the goods were not of satisfactory quality in that the said midi system was incorrectly wired.

(e) On 1 July 20__ and in consequence of the said breach the said midi system exploded when the claimant first attempted to use it.

(f) Further or in the alternative the explosion was caused by a defect in the said midi system supplied by the defendant in breach of s 2 of the Consumer Protection Act 1987.

(g) As a consequence of the explosion the claimant suffered loss and damage:
   - Particulars of special damage
   - Cost of the said stereo system damaged beyond repair £1,050.00

(h) In respect of any damages awarded to him the claimant is entitled to interest pursuant to s 69 of the County Courts Act 1984 for such periods and at such rates as to the court shall seem just.

The value of this claim does not exceed £5,000

AND the claimant claims:
   - £1,050 under paragraph 7 hereof
   - damages
   - interest as aforesaid

6.7.2 Supply of services

Particulars of claim

(a) At all material times the defendant carried on the business of painters and decorators.

(b) By an oral agreement made on 23 March 20__ the defendant by its office manager agreed to paint the front exterior of the claimant's house at 15 Acacia Avenue, Welltown for a price of £3,000.

(c) The defendant in the course of business painted the said house during the week commencing 18 April 20__. In the premises it was an implied condition that the defendant had to use reasonable care and skill.

(d) The defendant was in breach of the said condition, in that during the months from April to August 20__ the paint peeled off all the wooden surfaces of the front of the said house.

(e) In consequence of the said breach the claimant has suffered loss and damage:

- Particulars: Cost of scraping off the paint and repainting £1,250.00

(f) In respect of any damages awarded to him the claimant is entitled to interest pursuant to s 69 of the County Courts Act 1984 for such periods and at such rates as to the court shall seem just.

The value of this claim does not exceed £5,000

AND the Claimant claims:

- £1,250 under paragraph 5 hereof
- damages
- interest as aforesaid

6.8   Defence – precedents

6.8.1 Sale of goods

Defence (to 6.7.1)

(a) The defendant admits paras 1–3 inclusive of the Particulars of Claim.

(b) The defendant denies that it is in breach of the said implied condition as to the merchantability of the said midi system. The instruction book supplied with the goods stated that a 3-amp fuse should be inserted into the mains plug, but the claimant replaced it with a 13-amp fuse

(c) The defendant admits that the explosion occurred on 1 July 20__ as stated in para 5 of the Particulars of Claim, but denies that this was in consequence of a breach of contract as alleged. Further or in the alternative the said explosion was caused wholly or in part by the claimant's negligence.

(d) Para 6 of the Particulars of Claim is denied.

(e) In the circumstances the claimant is not entitled to recover the purchase price of the goods.

6.8.2 Supply of services

Defence (to 6.7.2)

(a) The defendant admits the facts stated in paras 1–3 inclusive of the Particulars of Claim.

(b) The defendant admits that the paint peeled off the house as alleged in para 4 of the Particulars of Claim, but denies that this was as a result of his breach of contract. The office manager referred to in the Particulars of Claim informed the claimant at the time the order was placed on 23 March 20__, that the old paint should be burnt off the wood at the front of the said house. In response to this information the claimant instructed the defendant merely to paint over the top of the said old paint.

(c) No admission is made as to the alleged loss or damage or as to any entitlement to interest as set out in paras 5 and 6 of the Particulars of Claim.

(d) In the circumstances, the claimant is not entitled to the relief claimed in part or at all.

6.9 Expert witnesses

Problems arising out of consumer goods may require opinions from technical experts, particularly as to the cause of a defect in a product. Suggestions for locating such experts are as follows:

(a) consult the advertisements in legal journals;

(b) consult *Yellow Pages* or other telephone directories to discover the names and addresses of trade associations (some are noted in Chapter 15), many are based in London, but not exclusively so;

(c) local libraries usually have a wide range of both trade and telephone directories, which will also assist in this research;

(d) trade magazines are also a useful source of information;

(e) the British Academy of Experts (for the address, see Chapter 15) has a register of qualified people.

Note that the Civil Procedure Rules restrict expert evidence to that which is reasonably required to resolve the proceedings (CPR 35.1). One solution to a consumer claim in this respect is to submit a particular issue through the ADR procedure to an expert agreed by both sides. That expert would then give his or her report.

6.10 Claimant's checklist

(a) Once a claim is established after interviews with the client and any witnesses (see paras 2.2 and 6.9), and there is no positive response from the prospective defendant then, subject to the client's instructions, draft a letter of claim. If the claimant is claiming damages as a result of personal injuries, follow the procedure set out in the Personal Injury Pre-Action Protocol.

(b) Send the letter of claim.

(c) Consider ADR, an offer to settle (CPR 36 and its associated Practice Direction) and pre-action disclosure (CPR 31.16) where, for example, disclosure of certain specified documents would be desirable to dispose fairly of the anticipated proceedings, or assist a resolution of the dispute without recourse to them, or would just save costs.

(d) Issue proceedings (CPR 7) in the appropriate court. Ensure that the claim form, statement of value, and the particulars of claim comply with the rules (CPR 16(1), 16(3) and 16(4), respectively). These must be verified by a statement of truth (CPR 22). Note the alternative procedure under r 8 should there be no substantial dispute of fact, but also note that a default judgment may not be obtained (CPR 12(2)(b)). In many cases, therefore, the procedure under r 7 will be more appropriate.

(e) Serve the proceedings within four months of issue (CPR 7.5), or apply for an extension (CPR 7.6).

(f) If the particulars of claim have not been included, these must be served within 14 days of service of the claim form (CPR 7.4). The particulars must include a form for defending the claim, a form for admitting it, and a form for acknowledging service (CPR 7.8(1)), although under r 8 only a form for acknowledging service need be sent.

(g) If there is a defence or counterclaim, file a reply at the same time as the allocation questionnaire issued by the court (CPR 15.8) and include a statement of truth. Consider issuing a request to stay proceedings for a month while ADR is tried (CPR 26.4(1)).

(h) If the defence raises questions, consider a request for further information (CPR 18).

(i) Consider an application for a summary judgment (CPR 24) if a defence on a particular issue has no realistic prospect of success. The parties must have 14 days' notice of the hearing date. If the respondent to the application wishes to rely on some written evidence at the hearing, he or she must serve the documents at least seven days before the hearing, and any evidence in reply must be served at least three days beforehand (CPR 24.5(2)). Note that the court can fix a summary judgment hearing of its own volition (CPR 24.5(3)).

(j) If the defendant has made a payment into court under r 36.10, consider accepting it. If final judgment is not better than such a payment, the claimant will have to pay the defendant's costs from the latest time the payment of offer could have been accepted (CPR 36.20).

(k) Some consumer claims will require the assistance of an expert witness or witnesses, but this procedure is restricted to 'that which is reasonably required to resolve the proceedings' (CPR 35.1). Note the general requirement of writing unless it is otherwise necessary (CPR 35.5). If an expert is required, apply to the court identifying the field on which the expert's evidence is to be relied (CPR 35.4(2)(a)) and, where practicable, the expert in the field (CPR 35.4(2)(b)). The expert's report must be accompanied by a statement of truth (CPR 35.10).

(l) Serve witness statements if necessary (CPR 32.4). Note that the court may order the party to serve such a statement or statements on the other parties to the case (CPR 32.4(2)). Witnesses in general must give oral evidence (CPR 32.5(1)).

(m) Note that the defendant should acknowledge service within 14 days of service of the claim (CPR 10.3(1)(b)), unless the particulars of claim are served separately. In that case, the acknowledgment should be 14 days from service of those particulars. The acknowledgment should be signed and include the address for service (CPR 10.5).

6.11 Defendant's checklist

(a) Consider an offer to settle before proceedings begin. Any offer must be open for 21 days and a prospective defendant must offer to pay the claimant's costs (CPR 36.10(2)). The court will take this into account if it has to make any order as to costs (CPR 36.10(1)).

(b) If the defendant knows that a claim form has been issued but not served, consider serving a notice on the claimant either to serve the form or to discontinue the action (CPR 7.7).

(c) Acknowledge service within 14 days after service of the claim form (CPR 10.3(1)(b)) unless the particulars of claim are served separately. In that case, the acknowledgment should be served within 14 days of the service of those particulars.

(d) File a defence (within 14 days of the statement of claim, or 28 days if an acknowledgment has been served, or 28 days by agreement (CPR 15.5(1)). The defence must comply with rr 16.5(a) and (b), that is, it must explain the reasons for the denial of any claim, it must state the allegations that the claimant has to prove and it must state which claims are admitted. The defendant must state a different version of events if he or she intends to put forward this (CPR 16.5(3)). Serve a counterclaim if required (CPR 22).

(e) File the allocation questionnaire provided by the court, and consider ADR (see para 6.10(g) above).

(f) Consider an application for an interim remedy, particularly the inspection of relevant property (CPR 25). Consumers are sometimes reluctant to allow even a reputable supplier of alleged faulty goods to examine them properly. It is therefore sometimes very difficult to discover whether goods are really faulty or if the consumer has misused them.

(g) If the case goes further, the court will allocate it to the appropriate track (CPR 26.5–26.8).

(h) Consider an application to require the claimant to provide more information (CPR 18).

(i) Consider an application for a summary judgment (see para 6.10(i) above).

(j) Consider a payment into court in respect of a money claim (CPR 36.10(3)). The payment must be made within 14 days of service of the claim form. If a claimant has made an offer in respect of a counterclaim consider accepting the offer.

(k) Experts: see para 6.10(k) above.

(l) Witnesses: see para 6.10(l) above.

6.12 Limitation of actions

(a) An action based on the breach of a simple contract must be brought within six years from the date on which the cause of action arose (s 5 of the Limitation Act (LA) 1980). This may be extended where the cause of action has been concealed by the defendant's fraud or where there has been a mistake. Time will then run from the time when the fraud or mistake could reasonably have been discovered (s 32 of the LA).

(b) Claims arising out of negligence, nuisance, breach of duty or under the Fatal Accidents Act 1976 must be brought within three years (ss 11 and 12 of the LA). Otherwise, in tort the period is six years.

(c) Actions relating to latent damage to property must be brought within three years of the time it could reasonably have been discovered subject to an absolute period of 15 years (s 14B of the LA).

(d) Actions in relation to defective products under the Consumer Protection Act 1987 must be brought within three years of time on which the cause of action accrued, or when the damage or injury was discovered. There is an absolute period of 10 years (s 11A of the LA).

(e) In cases of death, time runs from the date of death (s 12 of the LA).

(f) The court has a discretion to extend these time limits (other than the absolute periods) under s 33 of the LA.

6.13 Legal Aid

Complete the relevant forms, that is:

CLS MEANS 1–	means assessment form where the applicants are not receiving income support or income-based Jobseeker's Allowance
CLS MEANS1a–	self-employed
CLS MEANS1b–	partnership
CLS MEANS1c–	information about a shareholding in a private company or a directorship in one
CLSMEANS2–	means assessment form where the applicants are receiving income support or income-based Jobseeker's Allowance
CLSMEANS3–	where the main home is outside the UK
CLSMEANS4–	child under 16
CLSMEANS5–	change in capital

7 Consumer Credit – Consumers

7.1 Introduction

Problems arising out of the quality of goods are dealt with in Chapters 2–6, so this chapter is concerned with disputes affecting consumers in relation to the agreements themselves. The points made about interviewing the consumer-client made in Chapter 2 (para 2.1) are relevant to this area of law.

There is a difference in that the consumer is more often than not being sued for payments allegedly not made under the agreement. Some problems arise out of the consumer's right to cancel, but which is not accepted by the erstwhile lender's computer.

7.2 Consumers' questionnaire

(NB: the right hand side of the questionnaire must contain a column, so that the interviewer can highlight those areas where further and better particulars are needed. The questionnaire itself is designed for those clients who are being sued by hirers or creditors, but if they are having problems with specific areas such as with credit reference agencies, Chapter 9 should be consulted for guidelines.)

Client's name, date

Client's address

Brief summary of problem

If the problem arises out of a guarantee, name and address of the hirer or debtor

Name and address of the hirer or provider of the credit

Address of the registered office of the hirer or provider of credit

Name and address of the supplier of the goods and services

Address of the supplier's registered office (if a company)

Details of the information about the credit terms given to the creditor or hirer before the agreement was entered into

If a written quotation was given, brief details and dates

Date on which the consumer signed the consumer credit agreement

If the agreement was not made at the time the consumer signed the agreement, was a copy given to him or her at that time? YES/NO

When did the consumer receive a second copy of the agreement? NEVER/DATE

Place where the consumer signed the consumer credit agreement

Was this place other than at the premises of the creditor, owner, dealer or party to a linked transaction, and had oral representations been made to the consumer? YES/NO

If YES:

• had notice of cancellation been sent, or delivered, to the owner, hirer or creditor? YES/NO

• if such notice was, or alleged to be, sent or served, the date of service and if sent by post date of posting

Date on which the surety signed the agreement

If the client is a surety, does he or she have a copy of the agreement, and if so, when was it received?

Is the agreement governed by the Consumer Credit Act 1974? (see Chapter 9) YES/NO

Details of any ways in which the agreement does not conform with the provisions of the Act

Details of any promises or representations made to the client prior to the signing of the agreement

Was the subject matter of the agreement supplied in accordance with it? YES/NO

If the answer is NO, obtain details

Details of what went wrong

Chronology of complaints made by customer (including names of representatives of the creditor or hirer, supplier of the subject matter of the agreement, if known, as well as other bodies such as a trade association)

Details of correspondence with the creditor or hirer, supplier (if any) or other relevant people

Names and addresses of any witnesses who may be relevant

Note of instructions from the client

Legally aided? YES/NO

If YES, assist with completion of legal aid Green Form

If NO, obtain payment on account of costs

7.3   Follow-up

(a) Note the time taken at the interview.

(b) Draft a statement and send it to the client for approval.

(c) Follow up the unanswered relevant points in the questionnaire.

(d) If litigation is contemplated, send a letter next before action but, otherwise, write to the creditor or hirer in an attempt to resolve the problem.

(e) If the consumer is already being sued and is to dispute the claim, either serve a defence to the county court, or enter an appearance and instruct counsel.

(f) If the consumer is being sued and wishes to pay by instalments, complete the documents accordingly.

7.4   Letters – the right style

If the first approach is to be a letter with the objective of resolving the problem, the points made in Chapter 2 (para 2.5) must be noted.

8 Consumer Credit – Creditors

8.1 Introduction

Consumer credit is one area of law where creditors have to resort to litigation to enforce their rights. In order to do so, they have to observe a large number of rules affecting both the design of the form and procedures to be followed.

Problems arising out of the supply of goods and services are, however, covered in Chapters 2–5. The preliminary interview with the client should be the same as that mentioned in Chapter 3 (para 3.1).

8.2 Creditors' questionnaire

(NB: the right hand side of the questionnaire must contain a column for notes to assist in the follow-up. These will act as a reminder to obtain missing information such as letters from the consumer which the supplier has omitted to bring to the interview.)

Client's name, date

Client's address and telephone number

Name of contacts at the client's business

Brief summary of the problem

The name and address (including that of the registered office if it is a company) of the supplier of the goods or services under the agreement

Details of such goods or services

Details of any contract with the supplier of the goods and services

Is the agreement governed by the Consumer Credit Act 1974? (see Chapter 9) YES/NO

Details of the information about the credit terms given to the creditor or hirer before the agreement was entered into

If a written quotation was given, brief details and dates

Date on which the consumer signed the consumer credit agreement

If the agreement was not made at the time the consumer signed the agreement, was a copy given to him or her at that time? YES/NO

When was a second copy of the agreement sent to the consumer? NEVER/DATE

Place where the consumer signed the consumer credit agreement

Was this place other than at the premises of the creditor, owner, dealer or party to a linked transaction, and had oral representations been made to the consumer? YES/NO

If YES:

- had notice of cancellation been received by the owner, hirer or creditor? YES/NO

- if such notice was, or alleged to be, sent or served, the date of receipt and, if sent by post, date of actual or alleged posting

Name and address of surety (if any)

Did the surety sign the agreement? YES/NO

Date on which the surety signed the agreement

Was a copy of the agreement supplied to the surety? YES/NO

Chronology of any correspondence with the consumer

Details of any correspondence with third parties (for example, trade associations)

Details of any promises or representations made to the client prior to the signing of the agreement

Was the subject matter of the agreement supplied in accordance with it? YES/NO

If the answer is NO, obtain details

Details of what went wrong

Chronology of complaints made by customer (including names of representatives of the creditor or hirer, supplier of the subject matter of the agreement, if known, as well as other bodies such as a trade association)

Names and addresses of the client's employees who have had dealings with the consumer

Names and addresses of any other witnesses

Names and addresses of the suppliers' liability insurers and details of
any relevant insurance policy

Note of instructions from the client

Legally aided (sole traders only)? YES/NO

If YES, assist with the completion of legal aid Green Form

If NO, obtain payment on account of costs

8.3   Enforcement of the contract – procedure

If the debtor under a consumer credit agreement is late in paying, then
a default notice (s 87(1) of the Consumer Credit Act (CCA) 1974) must
be served before the creditor or owner can:

(a) terminate the agreement; or

(b) demand earlier payment of any sum; or

(c) recover possession of any goods or land; or

(d) treat any right conferred on the debtor or hirer by the agreement
as terminated, restricted or deferred; or

(e) enforce any security (note that a copy must be served on the surety
– see para 8.4 below).

There is no need to serve such a notice merely to inform a debtor that
any right to draw on credit is restricted or deferred. This is particularly
important in the context of credit cards, where their users go over their
credit limits or do not repay their debts.

The default notice must contain the following information (s 88 of
the CCA):

(a) the nature of the alleged breach;

(b) the action to be taken by the debtor or hirer to remedy it or, if it
cannot be remedied, the amount of compensation (if any) to be
paid;

(c) the date (which must be at least seven days from the date on which
the notice was served on the debtor or hirer) by which the breach
must be remedied or compensation paid; and

(d) the consequences for the debtor or hirer if the notice is ignored.

If it is ignored, then the creditor or owner can proceed to enforce the
agreement by following up one of the remedies mentioned in s 87(1)
of the CCA, provided that the agreement permits it.

If the debtor or hirer dies and the agreement is fully secured by, for
example, a charge over the goods, the procedure is governed by s 86 of

the CCA. The creditor or owner cannot do any of the things mentioned in s 87(1) of the CCA listed above, and the agreement is taken over by the personal representatives.

If the agreement is not fully secured, the creditor or owner can apply to the court, where it has to be proved that he or she is not satisfied that the present and future obligations are unlikely to be carried out (by the personal representatives of the late debtor or hirer). The creditor or owner can then obtain one of the rights listed in s 87(1), above.

Note that this does not apply to agreements of unspecified duration such as credit card arrangements. If these were that the debt would become immediately payable on the death of the debtor, such a provision would be enforceable.

8.4   Enforcement of the security – procedure

The full definition of security is contained in s 189(1) of the CCA and includes a guarantee. Once it is established that, for example, a guarantee is covered by the Act, then the procedure follows closely that mentioned in para 8.3 above.

A default notice (in the format detailed in SI 1983/1561 as amended by SI 1984/1109) must first be sent to the debtor or hirer. At the same time, a copy must be given to the surety, since failure to do so will mean that the security will be unenforceable without leave of the court (s 111 of the CCA). Note that if the main agreement itself is unenforceable the security also suffers the same fate (s 113 of the CCA) unless it is an indemnity in respect of a consumer credit agreement where the hirer or debtor was not of full age or capacity.

This may, however, be an infringement of the creditor's human rights (see Sched 1 to the Human Rights Act 1998 and *Wilson v First County Trust Ltd* [2001] 2 WLR 302, CA).

8.5   Recovery of the goods – procedure

If a debtor or hirer defaults, only the goods forming the subject matter of the consumer credit agreement will be of value to the hirer or creditor. They can only be reclaimed in limited circumstances. A court order, for example, will normally be needed, because the owner or creditor cannot enter any premises to take possession of the goods. If a hirer should retain them after the termination or expiration of an agreement, then the court will order their return with no option for payment as an alternative (s 100(5) of the CCA), unless it is just to order otherwise.

There are further restrictions in relation to what are defined as 'protected goods' under s 90 of the CCA 1974.

For this protection to apply:

(a) the debtor must be in breach of the agreement;

(b) one-third or more of the total price of the goods (excluding any installation charge which must have been cleared) has been tendered or paid to the creditor; and

(c) the property in the goods remains in the creditor.

Provided that the debtor has not disposed of the goods to a third party or abandoned them, the creditor cannot repossess the goods without a court order. The goods can, however, be handed over as the result of genuine negotiations between the creditor and debtor.

8.6 Follow-up (subject to the client's instructions)

(a) Note the time taken at the interview.

(b) Send a statement for the client's approval.

(c) Ensure both that the agreement is covered by the CCA 1974, and that its form complies with the Consumer Credit (Agreements) Regulations 1983 (SI 1983/1553, as amended by SI 1984/1109).

(d) Check that all procedures have been followed.

(e) If a default notice has not been served, prepare and serve the necessary documents.

(f) If a default notice has been served, commence litigation.

(g) Note that an application may be made to have the goods protected from damage by, say, delivery to a third party (s 131 of the CCA).

9 Consumer Credit – Common Problems

9.1 Applications by traders for licences

Professional firms will sometimes be asked to help new enterprises establish themselves in the credit business and an essential aspect of this is to obtain a licence from the Office of Fair Trading.

The categories are as follows:

A – consumer credit business

B – consumer hire business

C – credit brokerage

A licence is required whether or not the person seeking credit, or to hire goods, requires more than the £25,000 limit relating to the definition of a consumer credit agreement mentioned in more detail in para 9.5 below. Note that an otherwise sound consumer credit agreement made as a result of the introduction by an unlicensed credit broker may be unenforceable by the creditor or owner. Individuals may not canvass the services of a credit broker off trade premises. Credit brokers may not charge more than £3 for their fees where no credit agreement ensues within six months after the introduction by the broker. They cannot try and avoid the restrictions by restricting their agencies to foreign providers of finance for regulated agreements.

D – debt counselling and debt adjusting

Debt counsellors for this purpose are those who give advice in relation to liquidating debts due under a regulated consumer credit or hire agreement. Debt adjusters:

(a) negotiate on behalf of creditors or hirers terms for the discharge of their debts under such agreements;

(b) take over such obligations for a fee; or

(c) carry out similar activities in relation to the liquidation of debts under those agreements.

Some people are excepted and they include the creditor (who must not be an assignee other than one under the transfer of the business unless it is that of debt collecting) or hirer, supplier or credit broker. Group licences can be obtained for certain professional practices.

E – debt collecting

F – credit reference agency

Z – canvassing off trade premises

Many businesses will need a licence to cover more than one such category, while some businesses may need an extra authorisation to canvass for consumer credit business within the relevant category.

They will therefore have to observe the rules relating to such canvassing. It is an offence to seek debtor-creditor business this way, and debtor-creditor-supplier agreements may only be canvassed by the prospective creditor through its employees or agents or by means of a credit broker.

A consumer credit business can be summarised as the provision of credit not exceeding £25,000 to individuals. There are some exceptions and the more detailed flow chart in para 9.4 may be helpful.

Applications for licences should be made on Form CC1/93 for a consumer credit licence and for a group licence on Form CC3/7, which is obtainable from the Office of Fair Trading, whose address will be found in Chapter 15, or from local authority trading standards departments (often known by some councils as weights and measures or consumer protection departments).

Fees vary and applicants have to pay more for each category. Details should be obtained from the Office of Fair Trading.

The very act of registration means that there is a register which can be inspected. This should be checked if a consumer has been dealing with a creditor or hirer who appears to have been using doubtful methods to obtain payment. In any event, the Office of Fair Trading can refuse to register anyone who is not a 'fit person'.

A licence lasts for five years and is renewable. Reminders are fortunately sent out, but firms which provide company secretarial and administrative services for clients should note that changes must be notified to the Office of Fair Trading. These include changes or additions to trading names and to registered offices.

9.2   Credit reference agencies

As mentioned in para 9.1 above, credit reference agencies are a separate category (F). Their purpose is to provide information relevant to the financial standing of individuals, but consumers may need legal advice as a result of the information kept on the records of such agencies.

Problems arise out of incorrect information kept on file, so that a potential consumer is refused credit. If such a refusal is encountered, and it is suspected that a credit reference agency has been used, steps can be taken to see what is on file (s 159 of the Consumer Credit Act (CCA) 1974).

The full procedure is as follows:

(a) Within 28 days of the end of the negotiations for credit (that is, usually the refusal) the consumer may request the supplier to inform him or her of the name of the credit reference agency used.

(b) Within seven days, the supplier must disclose the name and address of such an agency (failure to comply is an offence).

(c) On payment of a fee of £1, the credit reference agency must within seven days of an application supply the enquirer with a copy of the information kept on its files about him or her together with a notice setting out the rights of the consumer in relation to correcting wrong details.

(d) If a consumer wishes to have the record corrected because of errors of fact prejudicing him or her, written notice may be served on the agency.

(e) The agency then has 28 days in which to serve a counter-notice of removal, amendment or non-action.

(f) If there is a counter-notice of removal, the agency must within 10 working days also give written notice to all customers to whom within the six months prior to receiving the consumer's original information about his or her financial standing has been given. This latter written notice must inform of the exact deletion if it was part of the original particulars given to the customers of the agency. If it was not part of such particulars, the agency must state that there has been a modification of the basis for its opinion of the consumer.

(g) A counter-notice of amendment must contain a copy of the corrected entry in the agency's file. It then has 10 days in which to notify its customers as in para (f) above.

(h) A counter-notice of non-action will be served where the credit reference agency is of the opinion that the information is correct or in its present form is not prejudicial to him or her.

(i) If the consumer is dissatisfied with the notice of amendment or of non-action, he or she can serve a notice of correction to be added to the agency's file. Such a notice must not exceed 200 words and must be correct. It must obviously comply with the laws relating to defamation, obscenity and blasphemy and must not display racial prejudice or be otherwise unsuitable.

(j) The credit reference agency has 28 days to give notice that it has complied with the notice of correction. It then has another 10 days to notify its customers in the same manner as mentioned in (f) and (g) above. If, however, the agency wishes to object to the notice, it has to apply on forms CC/314/77 and CC/315/77 to the Office of Fair Trading within the 28-day time limit. In these circumstances, a credit reference agency should be advised to negotiate an agreed notice of correction.

(k) If the credit reference agency should refuse to comply with the notice of correction the consumer may apply to the Office of Fair Trading. There are no special forms for this.

(l) If the Office of Fair Trading considers that the consumer is right, the agency will be directed to correct its records. If it fails to do so it will be liable to a fine on summary conviction of up to £1,000. Otherwise, the consumer's notice of correction may be quashed.

If a credit reference agency has been negligent in its recording or release of information to its clients and the consumer has suffered financial loss because of it, a claim for damages may be possible. Such businesses should have liability cover, so the matter may be resolved by negotiations with the insurance company.

9.3   Other incorrect information about consumers

Although incorrect information about consumers may be put right on the records of credit reference agencies, the creditor or hirer may keep its own information on file. It will then not be covered by the procedure mentioned in para 9.2 above.

If, however, the business refusing credit states that it has not consulted a credit reference agency, and the consumer suspects that the refusal is on the basis of incorrect information, the disclosure provisions of the Data Protection Act (DPA) 1999 may be helpful.

Data has a wide meaning and covers information 'processed by equipment operating automatically in response to instructions given for that purpose' (effectively computerised records) to a 'relevant filing system (that is, it includes manual records, too) (s 1(1) of the DPA). Personal data is information relating to an identifiable individual.

Consumers can make a request to a credit reference agency (s 7 of the DPA) but, unless that request shows a contrary intention, he or she is taken to have limited it 'to personal data regarding his financial standing'.

As in the case of credit reference agencies data controllers have to be registered (DPA, Pt III) and there are provisions for correcting or deleting incorrect information. Consumers have the right therefore to request on payment of a fee a copy of the information about them held by the data controller (s 7 of the DPA).

Requests for amendments may be made to the data user (s 10(1) of the DPA) and, if the consumer has suffered damage because of any inaccuracy, he or she is entitled to compensation for the damage and distress caused (s 13(1)of the DPA). Such claims may be pursued through the courts (s 15 of the DPA).

9.4   Types of agreement – flow chart

If not an exempt agreement, for example:

(a) mortgages;

(b) debtor/creditor/supplier agreements which finance land purchases and require more than four payments;

(c) certain fixed sum debtor/creditor/supplier agreements of four credit payments or less;

(d) running account debtor/creditor/supplier agreements where the credit provided in each payment is repayable in one amount (for example, American Express and Diners Club cards);

(e) debtor/creditor agreements where the rate of the total charge for credit does not exceed the higher of 13 per cent or one per cent above the highest bank base rate;

(f) trade agreements with foreign connections.

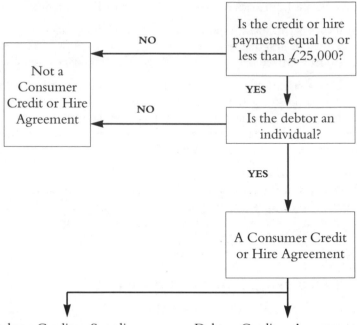

Debtor–Creditor–Supplier
    Agreements

Credit is advanced under pre-existing arrangements or in contemplation of future agreements between the creditor and the supplier, and either:

- the debtor is not free to choose how the credit is used, or

- the credit is advanced under pre-existing arrangements between the creditor and the supplier and in the knowledge that it is to finance a transaction between the debtor and the supplier.

Debtor–Creditor Agreement

Not a debtor–creditor–supplier agreement (see opposite)

9.5   Credit cards

Credit cards are another source of problems and are part of the definition of credit tokens in the CCA. Cash cards may also fall within the definition in the sense that the consumer may use it to overdraw his or her bank account.

The second copy of the agreement referred to in the questionnaires in Chapters 7 and 8 need not be provided until the consumer is given the credit card itself.

The problem relating to credit cards do not largely arise out of procedure. Instead, they relate both to the ease in which people sometimes seem to acquire them and the debt they consequently fall into, as well as to defects in the goods acquired with them. In the first instance, the professional adviser will try to help the client reorganise his or her affairs and to negotiate with the credit card company. The client may have to be advised to seek professional debt counselling. In the second case, the consumer may be able to sue that company instead of, say an insolvent retailer, because of s 75 of the CCA.

9.6   The agreement – checklist

The details of the form of the agreement are contained in the Consumer Credit (Agreements) Regulations 1983 SI 1983/1553 (as amended) which do not apply, among others, to small debtor-creditor-supplier agreements for restricted-use credit. There are, however, some points to look out for:

(a) there must be an informative heading;

(b) the names and addresses of the parties must be set out;

(c) description of the goods and services;

(d) the cash price;

(e) the amount of deposit or advance payment;

(f) description of any security provided;

(g) the amount of credit supplied (or the credit limit in the case of running account credit);

(h) the interest rate;

(i) the number, amount, frequency and timing of repayments;

(j) a reference to any further express terms (if any) in another document;

(k) a statement in the form set out in Sched 2 of SI 1983/1553 which sets out the debtor's statutory protection and remedies;

(l) the lettering must be legible and of a different colour from the paper;

(m) the terms must be shown together as a whole;

(n) the APR must not be shown less prominently than the cash price or other rate;

(o) the signature box must be in accordance with one of the layouts specified in Sched 5 to SI 1983/1553, but its purpose is to remind consumers that the agreement is governed by the CPA and that they should sign it only if they want to be bound by it.

10 Consumer Credit – Litigation

10.1 Which court?

For most purposes an action arising out of a consumer credit problem will be brought in the county court (see para 6.5 above).

10.2 Checklist for creditor/owner-claimants

Although the general principles as to most procedures and such matters as the drafting of pleadings remain the same as those for contract as mentioned in Chapter 5, there are some important differences. Litigation will usually be commenced by the creditor or owner, because the debtor or hirer will have paid only some or none of the payments due under the agreement. The procedure is as follows:

(a) Ensure that all default notices have been served on all the parties (see para 8.3 above).

(b) Draft particulars of claim, which must contain the details mentioned in para 10.3 below.

(c) If the action is to recover goods to which a regulated hire purchase agreement applies, commence action in the court for the district in which the debtor resides, or carries on business, or did so at the date when he or she made the last payment under the agreement (r 7.9 of the Civil Procedure Rules (CPR), Practice Direction, para 4).

(d) An application for a time order under s 129(1)(b) of the Consumer Credit Act (CCA) 1974 must contain the details mentioned in para 10.4 below (r 7.9 of the CPR, Practice Direction, para 7.3).

(e) If the creditor is not entitled to recover possession of the goods except by order of the court under s 90(1) of the CCA, an action to claim possession must be commenced (r 7.9 of the CPR, Practice Direction, para 7.8).

(f) An application for an order to enter premises in order to repossess goods under s 92(1) must be made by originating application (Sched 2 to the CPR, CCR Ord 49, r 4(13)).

10.3 Particulars of claims relating to the delivery of goods to enforce an HP or conditional sale agreement

These must contain the following details in the same order (r 7.9 of the CPR, Practice Direction, para 7.2):

(a) the date of the agreement;

(b) the parties to the agreement;

(c) the agreement number or other information to identify it;

(d) details of how the claimant came by the rights and duties of the creditor, if he or she was not an original party to the agreement;

(e) the place where the defendant signed the agreement if this is known;

(f) the goods claimed;

(g) the total price of the goods;

(h) the paid-up sum;

(i) the unpaid balance of the total price;

(j) the date and method of service of any default notice or notice under s 76(1) or s 88 of the CCA;

(k) the date on which the right to demand delivery of the goods arose;

(l) the cash amount claimed (if any) instead of delivery of the goods;

(m) any other amounts claimed.

10.4 Particulars of claims relating to a time order

These must contain the following details in the same order (r 7.9 of the CPR, Practice Direction, para 7.3):

(a) the date of the agreement;

(b) the parties to the agreement;

(c) the agreement number or other information to identify it;

(d) details of any sureties;

(e) details of how the claimant came by the rights and duties of the creditor, if he or she was not an original party to the agreement;

(f) the names and addresses of the persons intended to be served with the claim form;

(g) the place where the claimant signed the agreement;

(h) details of the notice served by the creditor or owner giving rise to the claim for the order;

(i) the total unpaid balance, and additionally the amount of any arrears (if known), as well as the amount and frequency of the payments as set out in the agreement;

(j) the claimant's proposal for payment and a statement of his or her means;

(k) if the claim relates to a breach of the agreement other than non-payment, the claimant's proposal to remedy it.

10.5 Precedent for consumers – claim arising out of the hirer's cancellation of agreement

Particulars of claim:

(1) On the 25th day of February 20__ the claimant entered into negotiations with the defendant with a view to acquiring a used car registration number G123 XYZ.

(2) During these negotiations the claimant agreed to accept the defendant's old banger, registration number ABC 123L, in part exchange at the price of £500 against the purchase price of £5,000 of the said used car.

(3) By an agreement number 123X in writing dated the 25th day of February 20__ the defendant agreed to let to the claimant the said used car on hire purchase subject to the terms and conditions set out in the said agreement. The claimant paid a deposit of £100 to the defendant.

(4) The said agreement was not signed at the defendant's place of business but at the claimant's home at 36 Rowan Avenue, Glastonberg on the 26th day of February 20__, so it was a cancellable agreement within the meaning of s 67 of the Consumer Credit Act 1974.

(5) The said old banger was delivered to the defendant's premises at 46 The High Street, Glastonberg, on the 26th day of February 20__.

(6) On the 3rd day of March 20__ the claimant received a copy of the said agreement in accordance with s 63 of the Consumer Credit Act 1974, and on that day served on the defendant notice cancelling the agreement pursuant to s 69 of the said Act.

(7) Despite requests the defendant has not delivered back to the claimant the said old banger nor repaid the said deposit.

(8) The claimant therefore claims:

(a) the deposit of £100;

(b) an order for the delivery up of the said old banger or the sum of £500;

(c) interest pursuant to s 69 of the County Courts Act 1984.

10.6 Precedent for creditors – recovery of possession of goods, unpaid instalments and minimum sum under a contractual term

Particulars of claim

(1) By an agreement, number 345Y, in writing dated the 25th day of March 20__ made between the claimant and the defendant and signed by the defendant at the premises of the claimant known as Dykeshop of The High Street, Glastontown, the claimant agreed to let to the defendant on hire purchase and subject to the terms and conditions therein contained a Dykeshop Midi System.

(2) By clause 9 of the said agreement the defendant agreed to pay an initial instalment of £65 and 36 monthly instalments of £28.05 payable on the first day of each month beginning on the 15th day of April 20__ and interest at a rate of 2 per cent per annum above the base rate of Berkland Bank plc on all instalments due and unpaid until the date of payment, and also to pay £1 on the exercise of the option to purchase the said Dykeshop Midi System.

(3) The hire purchase price of the said goods was £1,010.80. The defendant has paid the sum of £252.45 in respect of the said hire purchase price, and the amount of the unpaid balance is £758.35.

(4) On the 15th day of January 20__ the defendant failed to pay the instalment then due and on the 20th day of January 20__ the claimant served on the defendant a notice of default in pursuance of s 87 of the Consumer Credit Act 1974 stating the amount of the said instalment and requiring the said amount to be paid to the claimant within seven days of the service of the said notice.

(5) By the 27th day of January 20__ the defendant had failed to pay or tender the said or any amount, and the claimant was thereupon and is entitled under clause 11 of the said agreement to recover possession

and demand delivery of the said Dykeshop Midi System and to recover the amount by which one-half of the hire purchase price exceeds the total sums already paid and due under the said agreement [*or whatever is stipulated in the agreement*].

(6) The particulars required by the Civil Procedure Rules Pt 7 under Practice Direction – Consumer Credit Act Claim:

(a) The date of the agreement was 25 March 20__

(b) The Claimant and the Defendant are the parties to the agreement

(c) The agreement number is 345Y

(d) The agreement was signed at the Claimant's business premises known as Dykeshop, High Street, Glastontown

(e) The goods claimed are a Dykseshop Midi System

(f) The total price of the goods is £1,010.80

(g) The paid up sum is £252.45

(h) A default notice was served on the Defendant on 20 January 20__

(i) The date on which the right to demand delivery of the goods accrued on 27 January 20__

(j) As an alternative to delivery of the goods the Claimant claims £758.35

(k) The amount claimed in addition to the delivery of the goods are £28.05 being the arrears of instalments of rent together with contractual interest and £224.90 under paragraph of these Particulars of Claim

(7) At the date of the said agreement the claimant was the holder of a licence under s 21 of the Consumer Credit Act 1974.

AND the claimant claims:

(a) an Order for specific delivery of the said Dykeshop Midi System or alternatively £758.35 the unpaid balance of the hire purchase price;

(b) £28.05 arrears of instalments of rent, together with contractual interest thereon at the rate of 2 per cent per annum above the base rate of Berkland Bank plc, to the date hereof £__ and continuing at £__ a day;

(c) under paragraph 5 hereof £224.90 [*This is half of the unpaid £1010.80 less the sum of the paid amount (£252.45) and of the unpaid instalment (£28.05)*].

(d) Interest on all other sums due under the agreement or in the alternative under s 69 of the County Courts Act 1994.

10.7 Precedent – a defence for consumers – a defect in the documents

Defence

(1) The alleged agreement was a regulated agreement under the Consumer Credit Act 1974 purporting to be made by the claimants in the course of their business.

(2) The alleged agreement is not enforceable in that the defendant did not sign it as alleged in the Particulars of Claim and contrary to the Consumer Credit (Agreements) Regulations 1983 SI 1983/1553, para 6(1). An employee of the claimants showed the defendant a copy of the said agreement and said that it should not be signed until what he described as a credit check had been completed. No copy of the said agreement has ever been received by the defendant.

(3) In the premises the alleged agreement was not properly executed and the claimants are not entitled to enforce it.

10.8 Alternative to litigation

The Finance and Leasing Association (FLA) has an inexpensive conciliation and arbitration scheme to resolve disputes between FLA members and their customers. It applies to all agreements including those greater than the statutory £15,000 limit.

A code of practice has been set up in relation to the conduct of members, which states among other matters that they must all abide by the relevant legislation.

There are also useful procedural requirements, such as that the consumer should be made aware where appropriate of the availability of credit protection insurance. An FLA member also has to interview personally any credit broker, whose services that member proposes to use for the first time. Members must also be satisfied of any consumer's ability to pay.

The outline arbitration procedure is as follows:

(a) The Association refers any complaint to the chief executive of the FLA member about whom the complaint is made.

(b) If this is still not resolved, the Association will endeavour to conciliate between the customer and the member.

(c) If this fails the matter will normally be referred to a management committee.

(d) Otherwise there will be a binding arbitration under the FLA arbitration scheme operated by the Chartered Institute of Arbitrators.

(e) Neither (c) nor (d) is applicable where:

- the complaint relates to the commercial judgment of the FLA member as to the granting of credit facilities, etc;

- the complaint relates to the interest charged or to any other credit charges;

- the complaint arises out of any defect in, or unfitness of, the goods financed by the member, or out of any alleged misrepresentation or breach of contract by the supplier of the goods.

The Consumer Credit Trade Association has a similar scheme and procedure relating to its members. The topics not covered by its arbitration procedure relate to the commercial decision on whether to grant credit, to the rate of interest and to the quality of the goods.

The Consumer Credit Association also has an arbitration scheme, which is binding upon the parties, and is an alternative to litigation.

11 Unsolicited Goods and Services

11.1 Introduction

Members of the general public still have problems with unsolicited goods and services from time to time, and these are largely solved by reference to the Unsolicited Goods and Services Act (UGSA) 1971. This also has the important function of legislating against unsolicited advertising in its various guises.

11.2 Procedure – unsolicited goods

(a) The recipient of unsolicited goods must give them up to the sender during the period of six months beginning with the date of their receipt, but afterwards may deal with them as he or she likes (s 1(2)(a) of the UGSA). The goods, however, must have been sent with a view to their acquisition by the recipient (s 1(2) of the UGSA).

(b) Worried recipients may prefer to do something positive, in which case notice in writing may be sent to the sender not less than 30 days before the expiration of the six month period mentioned in the previous paragraph (s 1(2)(b) of the UGSA).

(c) The notice must be in writing and may be sent by post. It should contain the recipient's name and address, and where the goods may be repossessed if other than at that address. There must also be a statement that the goods are unsolicited (s 1(3) of the UGSA).

(d) The notice must give the sender at least 30 days to collect the goods (s 1(2)(b) of the UGSA).

(e) If the sender does not do so within the time limit, the recipient can deal with the goods as he or she wishes. The recipient must not unreasonably refuse the sender access to them within the 30 day or six month time limits.

11.3 Offences – unsolicited goods

A sender of unsolicited goods commits an offence if he or she demands payment in the course of any trade or business (s 2(1) of the UGSA). A fine of up to level 4 on the standard scale on summary conviction can be imposed. There is a defence if the sender has a reasonable belief that he or she has a right to payment.

There is potentially a greater fine of up to £400 if the recipient of unsolicited goods is threatened with legal proceedings, is placed on a list of defaulters, is the subject of any other collection procedure, or is threatened with the latter (s 2(2) of the UGSA).

Directors, managers, company secretaries or other similar officers of corporations are liable to prosecution, if they have connived in the commission of the offence.

11.4 Directories

Although the problem mainly affects businesses, individuals can be affected by the famous directory fraud, where invoices in respect of unrequested entries are sent and sometimes paid. Under s 3 of the UGSA, there is no liability for payment, and businesses which send out such demands for payment commit an offence punishable on summary conviction by a fine not exceeding the statutory maximum. Order forms must contain specific details (s 3(3) of the UGSA).

12 Consumer Safety – Defences for Suppliers

12.1 Introduction

The Consumer Protection Act (CPA) 1987 has introduced a new offence arising out of a failure to comply with a general safety standard (Pt II). There are also new defences, which must be considered while the client is being interviewed.

12.2 Questionnaire – breach of general safety standard

Name of the person being interviewed

Name and address of client

If the client is a company, the address of the registered office

Nature of the client's business

Brief details of the charge

Details of the goods alleged not to comply with the general safety requirement

Did the client manufacture the goods? YES/NO

If the answer is YES, did the problem arise out of a component of the goods? YES/NO

If the answer is YES:

Did the client manufacture the component? YES/NO

If the answer is YES, name and address of the supplier and details of the component

If the client did not manufacture the goods:

Was he/she/it an importer, wholesaler or retailer?

Name and address of the supplier

Date of purchase of the goods

Details of any contract of purchase (including terms as to quality and fitness for purpose of the goods)

Details of product information and instruction books provided by the supplier

Did the client intend the goods to be used or consumed in the United Kingdom? YES/NO

If the answer is NO, the client's reasons

Were the goods new? YES/NO

If the answer is YES:

Did the terms under which the goods were supplied or offered for sale indicate this? YES/NO

Did such terms provide for or contemplate that the goods would be supplied or to be supplied to the person or persons (ie, a consumer or consumers) in relation to the charge? YES/NO

If the client is a retailer:

Are the goods supplied in the course of a business supplying consumer goods? YES/NO

Have the goods previously been supplied in the United Kingdom? YES/NO

Details of any warnings or instructions supplied with the goods

Details of any costs that would have to be incurred to make the goods safe or to comply with the safety standard inferred by the charge

Details (including the date of publication) of any safety standard alleged to have been infringed by the client

Was the client aware of such safety standard?

Did the client comply with the safety standard? YES/NO

Details of the compliance or non-compliance

If the client did not comply with the safety standard, details of any belief by the client that the goods complied with the general safety standard

Details of any conflicting published safety standards

Details of any testing of the product by the client

Did the client supply, offer or agree to supply, or expose or possess any of the goods for supply as charged? YES/NO

If the answer is YES, the details are:

Names and addresses of any employees of the client who can give relevant evidence

12.3 Follow-up

(a) Send a statement to the client for approval.

(b) Obtain missing information as revealed by the questionnaire.

(c) Contact expert and other witnesses in order to obtain statements.

(d) Instruct counsel where required.

12.4 Offences under the Consumer Protection Act 1987

(a) Supplying, offering or agreeing to supply, or exposing or possessing, consumer goods which fail to comply with the general safety standard (s 10 of the CPA).

(b) Contravention of safety regulations made by the Secretary of State (s 12(1) of the CPA).

(c) Failing to carry out tests or procedures in accordance with those safety regulations in connection with the making or processing of goods with a view to ascertaining whether they satisfy such regulations (s 12(2)(a) of the CPA).

(d) Failing to deal or not to deal with a quantity of the goods in a particular way, of which the whole or part does not satisfy such a test or does not satisfy standards connected with such a procedure (s 12(2)(b) of the CPA).

(e) Failing to comply with a safety regulation which requires the provision of information, by means of a mark or otherwise, of specific information in relation to goods (s 12(3) of the CPA).

(f) Failing to give information without reasonable cause, or giving information either knowing it to be false or doing so recklessly, where such information is required under safety regulations to enable another to exercise his or her functions under them (s 12(4) of the CPA).

(g) Contravention of a prohibition notice, eg, by supplying goods which the supplier has been prohibited from doing by that notice, or a notice to warn, for example, by failing to supply a warning notice about the goods (s 13(4) of the CPA).

(h) Contravention of a Suspension Notice (s 14(6) of the CPA).

(i) Failure without reasonable cause to comply with a notice from the Secretary of State to provide information, or providing information knowing it to be false, or doing so recklessly (s 18(3) of the CPA).

(j) Intentional obstruction of an enforcement or customs officer acting in pursuance to Pt IV of the CPA (s 32(1)(a)).

(k) Intentional failure to comply with the requirement of an enforcement officer under Pt IV of the CPA (s 32(1)(b)).

(l) Failure to give any other assistance without reasonable cause to an enforcement officer acting under the provisions of Pt IV of the CPA (s 32(1)(c)).

(m) To make any statement under (l) above either knowing it to be false in a material particular, or being reckless in this respect, to an enforcement officer (s 32(2) of the CPA).

(n) Producers and distributors offering, or agreeing, to place on the market any dangerous product, or exposing or possessing any such product for placing on the market (reg 13(a) of the General Product Safety Regulations (GPSR) 1994 SI 1994/2328)).

(o) Producers or distributors offering or agreeing to supply any dangerous product, or exposing or possessing any such product for supply (reg 13(b) of the GPSR).

(p) Producers placing an unsafe product on the market (reg 12 of the GPSR).

(q) Distributors supplying products, which they know or should have presumed both on the basis of the information in their possession, and as professionals, are dangerous products.

12.5 Defences in respect of the general safety requirement

(a) Adequate instructions, warnings or markings (s 10(2)(a) of the CPA), but see s 12(3) in relation to specific safety requirements).

(b) Compliance with published safety standards (s 10(2)(b) of the CPA).

(c) The methods needed to make the goods safer were unreasonable or unreasonably expensive (s 10(2)(c) of the CPA).

(d) Compliance with 'any requirement imposed by or under any enactment or with any Community obligation' (s 10(3)(a)), but no higher standard is required (s 10(3)(b) of the CPA).

(e) Reasonable belief that the goods would not be used or consumed in the UK (s 10(4)(a) of the CPA).

(f) If a retailer and the goods were of a type normally acquired for private use or consumption (s 10(5) of the CPA) the accused neither knew nor had reasonable grounds for believing that the goods did not comply with the general safety requirement (s 10(4)(b) of the CPA).

(g) If the accused is a retailer, the goods were of a type normally acquired for private use or consumption, and the accused had indicated that the goods were not new and had not contemplated their actual or potential acquisition by the persons 'supplied or to be supplied' (s 10(4)(c) of the CPA).

(h) The goods are not consumer goods as defined in s 10(7) of the CPA – for example, they are not ordinarily intended for private use or consumption.

(i) The accused did not supply, offer or agree to supply, or expose or possess for supply the goods (s 10(1) of the CPA, and see s 12(1) in relation to specific safety regulations).

(j) The accused complied with the requirements of testing and dealing with the goods subsequent to such tests if this is the issue (s 12(2) of the CPA).

(k) Where false statements are an issue (see para 12.4(f) above) they were not false, or the accused did not know they were false, or he or she was not reckless in making them (s 12(4) of the CPA).

(l) Where an offence relates to breaches of prohibition notices, notices to warn and suspension notices, the offender did not in fact commit the alleged offence.

(m) Where the offence relates to the obstruction of enforcement officers (see para 12.4(j) to (l) above) such officers were not authorised, or the accused either had no intention to obstruct or comply or had reasonable cause in his or her failure to assist (s 32(1) of the CPA).

(n) Where the offence relates to false or reckless statements to enforcement officers (see para 12.4(m) above) the officers were not authorised, or such statements were not false, the accused did not make the statements recklessly or at all, or did not know that they were false (s 12(3) of the CPA).

(o) Due diligence (s 39(1) of the CPA), but where the defendant alleges that the offence was due to the act or default of another, or reliance on the information from another, not less than seven days' notice of the defence must be given. The court can give leave for a shorter period.

12.6 Penalties for offences in relation to the general safety requirement

(a) Breach of the general safety requirement (s 10(1) of the CPA) – on summary conviction a fine not exceeding level 5 on the standard scale, or a term of imprisonment not exceeding six months, or both (s 10(6) of the CPA).

(b) Offences against the safety regulations themselves (s 12(1) to (4) of the CPA – on summary conviction, a fine not exceeding level 5 on the standard scale, or a term of imprisonment not exceeding six months, or both (s 12(5) of the CPA).

(c) Offences in relation to prohibition notices, notices to warn, and suspension notices (ss 13 and 14 of the CPA) – on summary conviction a fine not exceeding level 5 on the standard scale, or a term of imprisonment not exceeding six months, or both (ss 13(4) and 14(6) of the CPA).

(d) Offences in relation to the obstruction of enforcement officers (s 32(1) of the CPA) – on summary conviction a fine not exceeding level 5 on the standard scale.

(e) Offences in relation to false or reckless statements made to enforcement officers (s 32(2) of the CPA – on summary conviction a fine not exceeding the statutory maximum (s 32(3)(a) of the CPA), but on conviction on indictment a fine (s 32(3)(b) of the CPA).

12.7 Appeals procedure – prohibition notices

(a) Representations must first be made in writing to the Secretary of State (CPA, Sched 2, para 2). If it is felt that an oral hearing and the evidence of witnesses will be helpful, then this should be stated in the light of the further procedure outlined below.

(b) If the Secretary of State after consideration of such representations decides not to revoke the notice, then a person must be appointed to consider them and any other representations including those of witnesses (CPA, Sched 2, para 2(1)(b)).

(c) Notification of a hearing date must be served, and such date must not be before the end of 21 days from the date of its service beginning with that day unless otherwise agreed (CPA, Sched 2, para 2(3)).

(d) As an alternative, the Secretary of State within one month beginning with the day he or she receives the written representations can in fact notify the trader that the prohibition notice shall stand as it is, be varied or revoked (CPA, Sched 2, para 3(2)). Only as an alternative may there be a hearing, in which case the procedure is the same as noted in (3) above (CPA, Sched 1, para 3(2)(b)).

(e) After an oral hearing a report is sent to the Secretary of State who may vary or revoke the notice (CPA, Sched 1, para 5(1)) but any variation may not be more restrictive than the original (CPA, Sched 1, para 5(2)).

12.8 Appeals procedure – notices to warn

(a) Within 14 days of the service of the draft notice (beginning with the date of service) inform the Secretary of State of the intention to make representations and whether or not they will be made orally, in writing or both (CPA, Sched 2, para 6(1)(e)).

(b) If such representations are to be made in writing this must be done within 28 days from the date of service of the draft notice beginning with the date of service (CPA, Sched 2, para 7(1)(b)).

(c) If oral representations are to be made, the person on whom the draft notice is served will be informed of the time and place of the hearing. This will be not before the end of the 28-day period mentioned in (b) above and also not before a further seven days beginning with the date on which the recipient of this information actually receives it (CPA, Sched 2, para 7(3)). The Secretary of State may notify a later time or times (CPA, Sched 2, para 10(1)).

(d) If there is an oral hearing witnesses may be called (CPA, Sched 2, para 7(4)).

(e) After the oral hearing a written report is sent to the Secretary of State, who may serve the proposed notice with or without modifications (but any revised notice must not be more onerous than the original one) (CPA, Sched 2, para 8(2) to (4)) or withdraw it (CPA, Sched 2, para 9).

12.9 Appeals against suspension notices

(a) An application to set out such an order must be made by the person who has an interest in the goods subject to the order (s 15(1) of the CPA).

(b) The application must be made to the magistrates' court either where proceedings have been brought for a contravention of a safety provision in relation to the goods or for their forfeiture (s 15(2) of the CPA). If there are no such proceedings then the application may be made to any magistrates' court.

(c) An appeal from the decision of the magistrates' court may be made to the Crown Court (s 15(5) of the CPA).

Note that in *R v Birmingham City Council ex p Ferrero Ltd* (1993) 1 All ER 530, it was suggested that a local authority is under no duty to consult a trader either before or after the service of a suspension notice.

12.10 Forfeiture of goods – procedure

(a) An application for an order for the forfeiture of goods may be made by an enforcement authority to a magistrates' court on the grounds that a safety provision in relation to the goods has been contravened (s 16(1) of the CPA).

(b) The proper magistrates' court is;

- where proceedings have already been brought in respect of a contravention of a safety provision in relation to some or all of the goods; or

- where an application in relation to a suspension notice concerning the goods has been made; or

- where an appeal application in respect of their detention has been made.

In the absence of any of these, then the application may be made to any magistrates' court (s 16(2) of the CPA).

(c) Note that although the court can make the order where it is satisfied that there has been a contravention in relation to the goods of a safety provision (s 16(3) of the CPA), it can do so where the goods are merely representative of goods contravening such a provision (s 16(4) of the CPA).

(d) An appeal lies to the Crown Court (s 16(5) of the CPA).

(e) The court may order the goods to be destroyed (s 16(6) of the CPA) or released to someone for scrapping or repair provided that the costs of forfeiture are paid (s 16(7) of the CPA).

12.11 Detention of goods – appeal procedure

(a) An application to set out such an order must be made by the person who has an interest in the goods subject to the order (s 33(1) of the CPA).

(b) The application must be made to the magistrates' court either where proceedings have been brought for a contravention of a safety provision in relation to the goods or for their forfeiture (s 33(2) of the CPA). If there are no such proceedings then the application may be made to any magistrates' court.

(c) The goods will be released if no such proceedings have been brought and more than six months have elapsed since the goods were seized (s 33(3) of the CPA). Compensation may be payable by the enforcement authority (s 34(1) of the CPA).

(d) An appeal from the decision of the magistrates' court may be made to the Crown Court (s 33(4) of the CPA).

13 False Price Indications – Defences for Suppliers

13.1 Introduction

The principles of the law relating to prices are to be found in the Consumer Protection Act (CPA) 1987, but more specific provisions are contained in various statutory instruments. The following are particularly important.

(a) The Consumer Protection (Code of Practice for Traders on Price Indications) Approval Order 1988 SI 1988/2078. One of its purposes is to give 'practical guidance with respect to the requirements of s 20 of the Consumer Protection Act 1987'.

(b) The Price Indications (Method of Payment) Regulations 1991 SI 1991/199.

(c) The Price Marking Order 1999 SI 1999/3042. Its main purpose is to implement the European Parliament Directive 98/6/EC.

13.2 Questionnaire

Name of the person being interviewed

Name and address of client

If the client is a company, the address of the registered office

The nature of the client's business

Brief details of the problem

Date on which the offence was alleged to have been committed

To which goods, services, facilities or accommodation did the allegedly
misleading price indication relate?

Summary of the facts on which the charge is formulated

If the same prices have been quoted at other branches of the client,
details of the branches and the length of time that the offer has been
open

If the prices were quoted by reference to other suppliers in relation to
goods or services of the same description, such supplier's name and
address, details of its pricing structure, source of information and
the reasons for believing that this was the situation current at the
time of the commission of the alleged offence

If the price indication included a comparison with other goods of the
same description, were there any differences in the two types of
goods and, if so, what were they?

Were the prices indicated to consumers (see s 20 of the CPA 1987)

What procedure did the client follow in framing the price indication?

Was the price indication made in accordance with any such procedure?

Which person actually displayed the price indication?

Was such a person acting under the instruction of another employee,
owner or director of the firm and, if so, what are the details?

Details of any code of practice relating to the prices in question

Names and addresses of any employees of the client who can give relevant
evidence

13.3 Follow-up

(a) Send a statement to the client for approval.

(b) Obtain missing information as revealed by the questionnaire.

(c) Contact expert and other witnesses in order to obtain statements.

(d) Instruct counsel where required.

13.4 Some points to watch out for

The Consumer Protection (Code of Practice for Traders on Price
Indications) Approval Order 1988 SI 1988/2078 is a guide to the various
means by which shopkeepers and mail order businesses promote their
products through price comparisons, special offers and the like. Note
that transgression of the code will not of itself give rise to any civil or

criminal liability (s 25(2) of the CPA), but it will be evidence of a breach of s 20 of the CPA.

The following points are particularly important:

(a) There are detailed rules relating to price comparisons with the trader's previous price for the same product. Both must be shown, and the goods must have been available to consumers at the previous higher price for at least 28 consecutive days in the previous six months. If the higher price was available at a different store, then this must be clearly set out. Note the exception that the previous price may be 'the last price at which the goods were on sale in the previous six months and applied in the same shop where the reduced price is being offered' where those goods are food and drink or non-food perishables with a shelf life of less than six weeks.

(b) Introductory price offers may only be made where there is an intention to offer the product for sale at a higher price after the offer period is over. Such periods must not be so long as to be misleading, although they may be extended provided that this is clearly indicated.

(c) Comparisons with another trader's prices must identify that business accurately.

(d) It seems as though every manufacturer who suggests Recommended Retail Prices has encouraged every retailer to offer the products at lower prices. Note, however, that those retailers must have dealt with the supplier on normal commercial terms.

(e) Items purchased specially for Sales must be indicated as such.

(f) Another price indication that can cause confusion at Sales is a general statement, such as 'up to 50% off' but that maximum reduction must apply 'to at least 10% (by quantity) of the products on offer'.

(g) Although VAT exclusive prices may be quoted, prominent statements must be displayed that VAT at a quoted percentage is to be added. Changes in the VAT rate can make prices misleading, so they must be made clear to any consumer before they buy the product.

(h) Restaurant service charges must be incorporated in a fully inclusive price wherever practicable.

(i) The consumer must be made aware of any call-out charges.

(j) Price indications in newspapers and magazines should apply for a reasonable period, such as seven days or up to the next issue of the publication.

(k) Note that the Price Indications (Method of Payment) Regulations 1991 SI 1991/199 deal with goods other than fuel.

(l) In *Allen v Redbridge LBC* (1994) 1 WLR 139, it was said that Parliament had not intended to lay down the precise means by which a retailer should notify the public of the price of goods. The retailer had complied with the Price Marking Order, even where the prospective purchaser could only see the prices of expensive perfumes with the help of a shop salesperson.

(m) Traders must generally indicate selling prices by units of weight, for example, grams, as listed in Sched 2 to the Price Marking Order 1999 SI 1999/3042. There are some minor exceptions for small shops and vending machines, etc (Art 5).

13.5 Defences – the Consumer Protection Act 1987

(a) The price indication was not misleading (ss 20(1) and 24(4) of the CPA). The test is what the consumer might reasonably infer in relation to the various matters mentioned in s 21 of the CPA. They include the expectation that the price is less than it is, that it does not depend on facts or circumstances on which it depends, and that it covers matters for which an extra charge is made (s 21(1)(a) to (c) of the CPA). Others are the lack of expectation that the price is to be increased or reduced in particular circumstances (s 21(1)(d) of the CPA). Similar considerations in relation to reasonable inferences apply to methods of determining a price (s 21(2) of the CPA) and price comparisons (s 21(3) of the CPA). Note that the Act is not directed against employees (*R v Warwickshire CC ex p Johnson* (1993) 2 WLR 1).

(b) Where the price indication has subsequently become misleading, it was not reasonable to expect that any consumer would be expected to rely on the indication at that time, or that reasonable steps had been taken to prevent such consumers from relying on the indication (s 20(2) of the CPA).

(c) The prosecution has been brought outside the relevant time limits. They are the earlier of the end of three years beginning with the day of the commission of the offence, or the end of one year beginning with the day that the prosecutor discovered that the offence had been committed.

(d) The price indication was made in accordance with the regulations made by the Secretary of State under s 26 of the CPA 1987 (s 24(1)). Such regulations may, of course, bring in new defences.

(e) Although the price indication was contained in a publication or a broadcast, it was not in an advertisement (s 24(2) of the CPA).

(f) A person who publishes or arranges the publication of an advertisement is not liable, provided that it was received for publication in the ordinary course of business, and that he or she did not know, or could not have suspected, that it contained a misleading price indication.

(g) Compliance with a code of practice approved by the Secretary of State under s 25 of the CPA 1987.

14 Misleading Trade Descriptions – Defences for Suppliers

14.1 The offence in relation to goods

In the course of a trade or business the Trade Descriptions Act (TDA) 1968 makes it an offence to apply a false trade description to goods, or to supply or offer to supply such goods (s 1(1) of the TDA). The definition of trade description is very wide (s 2(1) of the TDA) and relates to:

(a) quantity, size or gauge;

(b) method of manufacturing, producing, processing or reconditioning;

(c) composition;

(d) fitness for purpose, strength, performance, behaviour, or accuracy;

(e) any other physical characteristics;

(f) testing by any person and the results;

(g) approval by any person and the results;

(h) place or date of manufacture, production, processing or reconditioning;

(i) person by whom manufactured, produced, processed or reconditioned;

(j) other history including previous ownership or use.

A trade description, as well as being made orally (s 4(2) of the TDA) can include marks on the goods, information supplied with them, and the packaging (s 4(1) of the TDA). It may also be made when goods are supplied 'in pursuance of a request in which a trade description is used and the circumstances are such as to make it reasonable to infer that the goods are supplied as goods corresponding to that trade description, the person shall be deemed to have applied that trade description to the goods'.

14.2 The offence in relation to services, accommodation or facilities

It is an offence to make false or reckless statements in relation to services, accommodation or facilities (s 14 of the TDA). In the course of a trade or business they relate to the provision or nature of any services etc (s 14(b)(i) and (ii) of the TDA). In other instances, they concern the time at which, manner in which, or persons by whom they are provided (s 14(b)(iii) of the TDA). False trade descriptions can also be made about the examination, approval, or valuation of the services, etc (s 14(b)(iv of the TDA)) as well as the location or amenities of any accommodation (s 14(b)(v) of the TDA).

14.3 Questionnaire

Name of the person being interviewed

Name and address of client

If the client is a company, the address of the registered office

The nature of the client's business

Brief details of the problem

Date on which the offence was alleged to have been committed

Place where the offence was alleged to have been committed

To which goods, services, accommodation or facilities did the allegedly false trade description relate?

How was the allegedly false trade description made?

Summary of the facts on which the charge is formulated

Do these indicate that the trade description is false to a material degree (s 3(1) of the TDA)?

Which person made the allegedly false trade description?

Was such a person acting under the instruction of another employee, owner or director of the firm and, if so, what are the details?

Was the allegedly false trade description made as a result of information supplied by someone else and, if so, what are the details? Details of any code of practice or statutory provisions relating to the goods in question

Names and addresses of any employees of the client who can give relevant evidence

14.4 Follow-up

(a) Send a statement to the client for approval.

(b) Obtain missing information as revealed by the questionnaire.

(c) Contact expert and other witnesses in order to obtain statements.

(d) Instruct counsel where required.

(e) If the defence is that the alleged act or default is that of some other person, serve at least seven days' notice in writing to the prosecutor (s 24(2) of the TDA).

14.5 Defences

(a) The statement about the provision or nature of services, accommodation or facilities was not made in the course of a trade or business (s 14 of the TDA).

(b) The statement was true.

(c) The person making the statement neither knew it was false nor was reckless (s 14 of the TDA). In relation to the charge of supplying or offering to supply goods to which a false trade description has been given, there is the defence that the person making it did not know, nor could with reasonable diligence have ascertained that they did not conform to the description (s 24(3) of the TDA).

(d) The time limits for bringing the charges have expired. On indictment this is the earlier of three years from the discovery of the offence or one year from the discovery by the prosecutor (s 19(1) of the TDA). In respect of magistrates' courts the time limit is 12 months within the commission of the offence (s 19(4) of the TDA) except in the case of oral statements where the time limit is six months (s 127 of the Magistrates' Courts Act 1980).

(e) The offence is due to the fault of another person (s 23 of the TDA). As noted in the previous chapter, this has proved to be a popular defence, but directors, managers, company secretaries or other similar officers of corporations can be found guilty of an offence, if they consented or connived at the making of the false trade description (s 20 of the TDA).

(f) The statement was made by mistake, as a result of reliance on information supplied by another person, or due to some other cause beyond the control of the person making it. Anyone seeking to use this defence must also show that he or she took all reasonable precautions, and exercised all due diligence to avoid the commission of such an offence by himself or herself or any person under his or her control (s 24(1) of the TDA).

(g) In relation to advertising containing a false trade description, innocent publication is a defence (s 25 of the TDA).

(h) Definition Orders (s 7 of the TDA) Marking Orders (s 8 of the TDA) or the rules in relation to what should be used in advertising (s 9 of the TDA) all issued by the Board of Trade, were complied with.

15 Useful Names and Addresses

Advertising

Advertising Standards Authority
2 Torrington Place
London
WC1E 7HW
Tel: 020 7580 5555
Fax: 020 7631 3050
Web: http://www.asa.org.uk

Institute of Practitioners in
Advertising
44 Belgrave Square
London
SW1X 8QS
Tel: 020 7235 7020
Fax: 020 7245 9904

Arbitration

The Chartered Institute of
Arbitrators
International Arbitration Centre
24 Angel Gate
326 City Road
London
EC1V 2RS
Tel: 020 7837 4483
Fax: 020 7837 4185
Web:
http://www.arbitrators.org

Chemists

The National Pharmaceutical
Association
Mallinson House
38–42 St Peter's Street
St Albans
Herts
AL1 3NT
Tel: 01727 832161
Fax: 01727 840858
Web: http://www.npa.co.uk

Consumer Associations

Consumers in Europe Group
20 Grosvenor Gardens
London
SW1W 0DH
Tel: 020 7881 3021
Fax: 020 7730 8540
Web: http://www.ceg.co.uk

The Consumers' Association
2 Marylebone Road
London
NW1 4DF
Tel: 020 7770 7000
Fax: 020 7770 7600
Web: http://www.which.net

The National Association of
Citizens' Advice Bureaux
115 Pentonville Road
London
N1 9LP
Tel: 020 7883 2181
Fax: 020 7833 4371
Web: http://www.nacab.org.uk

The National Consumer
Council
20 Grosvenor Gardens
London
SW1W 0DH
Tel: 020 7730 3469
Fax: 020 7730 0191
Web: http://www.ncc.org.uk

The Welsh Consumer Council
5th Floor, Longcross Court
47 Newport road
Cardiff
CF2 1WL
Tel: 01222 255454
Fax: 01222 255464
Web: http://www.
wales.consumer.org.uk

Consumer Credit

Birmingham Settlement Money
Advice Centre
318 Summer Lane
Birmingham
B19 3RL
Tel: 0121 3593562
Fax: 0121 3596357

The Consumer Credit Trade
Association (CCTA)
1st Floor
Tennyson House
159–63 Great Portland Street
London
W1N 5FD
Tel: 020 7636 7564
Fax: 020 7323 0096

Finance & Leasing Association
Imperial House
15–19 Kingsway
London
WC2B 6UN
Tel: 020 7836 6511
Fax: 020 7420 9600
Web: http://www.fla.org.uk

This advice centre helps people
sort out their financial affairs.

Consumer Credit Association of
the UK
Queens House
Queens Road
Chester
CH7 3BQ
Tel: 01244 312044
Fax: 01244 318035

Retail Credit Group
Kings Court
2–16 Goodge Street
London
W1P 1FF
Tel: 020 7580 8715
Fax: 020 7436 5062

Electricity and Gas

Various Councils will be established in various parts of England and Wales

Office of Gas & Electricity Markets (OFGEM)

130 Wilton Road
London
SW1V 1LQ
Tel: 020 7828 0898/0800 887777
Fax: 020 7932 1600
Web: http://www.ofgem.gov.uk

Electrical Installations

National Inspection Council for Electrical Installation Contracting
Vintage House
37 Albert Embankment
London
SE1 7UJ
Tel: 020 7564 2323
Fax: 020 7564 2370

Experts

British Academy of Experts
2 South Square
Grays Inn
London
WC1R 5HT
Tel: 020 7637 0333
Fax: 020 7637 1893
Web: http://www.academy-experts.org

Government Departments

Department of Trade and Industry
Consumer Affairs Division
10–18 Victoria Street
London
SW1H 0NN
Tel: 020 7215 5000
Fax: 020 7222 9280
Web: http://www.dti.gov.uk

HM Customs and Excise
South Bank Business Centre
Dorset House
Stamford Street
London
SE1 9PY
Tel: 020 7865 4400
Fax: 020 7202 4595
Web: http://www.hmce.gov.uk

Ministry of Agriculture Fisheries and Food
17 Smith Square
London
SW1P 3JR
Tel: 020 7238 3000
Fax: 020 7238 6591
Web: http://www.maff.gov.uk.org

The Office of Fair Trading
Fleetbank House
2–6 Salisbury Square
London
EC4Y 8JX
Tel: 020 7211 8000
Fax: 020 7211 8800
Web: http://www.oft.gov.uk

Health

Health Development Agency
Trevelyan House
30 Great Peter Street
London
SW1P 2HW
Tel: 020 7222 5300
Fax: 020 7413 8900
Web: http://www.hda-online.org.uk

Laundry

The Textile Services Association
7 Churchill Court
58 Station Road
North Harrow
Middlesex
HA2 7SA
Tel: 020 8863 7755
Fax: 020 8861 2115

Home Laundering Consultative
Council
5 Portland Place
London
W1N 3AA
Tel: 020 7636 7788
Fax: 020 7636 7515

Mail Order

Mail Order Traders' Association
40 Waterloo Road
Birkdale
Southport
PR8 2NG
Tel: 01704 563787
Fax: 01704 551249

Mail Order Protection Scheme
Queens House
28 Kingsway
London
WC2B 6JR
Tel: 020 7404 4166
Fax: 020 7404 4767
Web: http://www.ppa.co.uk

Motor Vehicles

Vehicle Builders and Repairers
Association
Belmont House
102 Finkle Lane
Gildersome
Leeds
LS27 7TW
Tel: 0113 2538333
Fax: 0113 2380496
Web: http://www.vbra.co.uk

Society of Motor Manufacturers
and Traders Limited
Forbes House
Halkin Street
London
SW1X 7DS
Tel: 020 7235 7000
Fax: 020 7235 7112

Post Office

The Post Office Users' National
Council
6 Hercules Road
London
SE1 7DN
Tel: 020 7928 9458
Fax: 020 7928 9076
Web: http://www.pounc.org.uk

The Post Office Users' Council
for Wales
Caradog House
St Andrews Place
Cardiff
CF1 3BE
Tel: 01222 374028
Fax: 01222 668536
Web: http://www.poucw.org.uk

Product Quality

The British Standards Institution
389 Chiswick High Road
London W4 4AL
Tel: 020 8996 9000
Fax: 020 8996 7400
Web: http://www.bsi.org.uk

Travel

The Air Transport Users
Council
CAA House
45–49 Kingsway
London
WC2B 6TE
Tel: 020 7240 6061
Fax: 020 7240 7071
Web: http://www.auc.org.uk

The Association of British
Travel Agents
68–71 Newman Street
London
W1P 4AH
Tel: 020 7637 2444
Fax: 020 7637 0713
Web: http://www.abtanet.com

Water

Office of Water Services
Centre City Tower
7 Hill Street
Birmingham
B5 4UA
Tel: 0121 625 1300
Fax: 0121 625 1400
Web: http://www.
open.gov.uk/ofwat

16 Further Reading

Title	Author	Publisher
The Law of Consumer Protection and Fair Trading	Harvey, BW and Parry, DL	Butterworths
Chitty on Contracts	Beale, H (ed)	Sweet & Maxwell
The Civil Procedure Rules in Action	Grainger, I and Fealy, M	Cavendish Publishing
Clerk & Lindsell on Torts	Brazier, M and Dugdale, T (eds)	Butterworths
Consumer Credit Law & Practice	Goode, R (Sir) (General ed)	Butterworths
County Court Precedents		Butterworths
Encyclopedia of Consumer Credit Law	Guest, AG and Lloyd, MG	Sweet & Maxwell
Product Liability & Safety Encyclopedia	Miller, CJ	Butterworths
Trading & Consumer Law (looseleaf)	Various	Butterworths

It is also important to keep up to date with the changing legal scene, and useful articles appear in:

Journal of Business Law	Sweet & Maxwell
New Law Journal	Butterworths
Solicitors Journal	FT Law & Tax

It is useful to know how salespeople use techniques of persuasion, and the following book is helpful:

Compelling Selling	Lund, PR	Macmillan